# Bloom Where You're Planted

## Reflections on Servant Leadership

*By*

## Dr. Crystal J. Davis

*Foreword by*

## Jeff Miller, Ph.D.

To Becky and Val -
Blessings
On Your Servant
Leadership Journey!
Dr. Crystal
So nice to meet you!
#TeamCloud

*Crystal J. Davis*

CJD Consulting Solutions, LLC
PO Box 141
Junction City, KS 66441
(785) 317-0045

**Copyright © 2018 Crystal J. Davis**

*Crystal J. Davis*

DEDICATION

To Elijah,
Thank you for choosing me to be your Mom

# *Thank you!*

# DOWNLOAD THE
# PODCAST
# FREE!

**READ THIS FIRST**

Just to say thanks for buying my book, I would like to gift you an interview with me and the **First and Foremost Podcast** 100% FREE!

**TO DOWNLOAD GO TO:**

Podcast, Dr. Crystal J. Davis on Bloom Where You Are Planted

**HTTPS://ITUNES.APPLE.COM/US/PODCAST/BLOOM-WHERE-YOU-ARE-PLANTED/ID1296644200?I=1000419466921&MT=2**

*Crystal J. Davis*

## CONTENTS

*Foreword* by Jeff Miller                                          9

*Acknowledgments*                                                 13

*The Back Story*                                                  15

**Essays, Seven Pillars of Servant Leadership: Practicing the
Wisdom of Leading by Serving by James W. Sipe and
Don M. Frick**

1  Servant Leadership and Character                               19

2  Servant Leadership and Putting People First                    22

3  Servant Leadership and Skilled Communication                   24

4  Servant Leadership and Compassionate Collaboration             27

5  Servant Leadership and Foresight                               31

6  Servant Leadership and Systems Thinking                        35

7  Servant Leadership and Moral Authority                         38

**Essays, The Speed of Trust: The One Thing That Changes
Everything by Stephen M. R. Covey**

8  Servant Leadership and Trust                                   41

9  Servant Leadership and Self-Trust                              44

10  Servant Leadership and Relationship Trust                     47

11  Servant Leadership and Organizational Trust                   51

12  Servant Leadership and Market Trust                           56

13  Servant Leadership and Societal Trust                    59

14  Servant Leaders and Global Citizenship                   62

15  Servant Leadership and Inspiring Trust                   65

16  Servant Leadership and Extending Smart Trust             67

17  Servant Leadership and Restoring Trust                   70

18  To Trusting Again                                        75

19  A Propensity to Trust                                    78

**Essays, A Force for Good: The Dalai Lama's Vision for Our World by Daniel Goleman**

20  A Force for Good                                         81

21  Reinvent the Future                                      86

22  Emotional Hygiene                                        89

23  The Kindness Revolution                                  94

24  Partnering with Science                                  99

25  A Muscular Compassion                                    102

26  Economics as if People Mattered                          105

27  Care for Those in Need                                   109

28  Heal the Earth                                           113

29  Three Ways to Create a World that Works for Everyone     117

30  Four Ways to Educate the Heart                           120

31  Servant Leadership and the Long View                     124

32  Act Now                                                  126

**Essay, Authentic Conversations: Moving from Manipulation to Truth and Commitment by Jamie Showkeir and Maren Showkeir**

33 Servant leadership and Authentic Conversations 129
**Essay, Start with Humility: Lessons from America's Quiet
CEO's on How to Build Trust and Inspire Followers
by Merwyn Hayes and Michael Comer**

34 Servant Leadership: Humility, Confidence, and Crucible Moments 133

35 Lead. From, Within Blog: 2015 Year in Review 136

**Essays, Practicing Servant Leadership: Succeeding
through Trust, Bravery, and Forgiveness by Larry C. Spears
and Michelle Lawrence**

36 Who Is a Servant-Leader? 139

37 Six Applications of Servant Leadership 142

38 Four Ways Boards of Directors Use Servant Leadership 148

39 Six Qualities of a Board Chair as Servant-Leader 153

40 Three Questions to Consider as a Servant-Leader 158

41 Ten Core Competencies of Servant Leadership and
Philanthropic Institutions 161

42 Four Values of Servant-Led Organizations 165

43 Eleven Tips for Servant-Led Collaborations 168

44 The Eight Pitfalls of Organizations and Emerging
Servant Leaders 172

45 Six Positive Phrases Servant-Leaders Use When Listening 175

46 Four Premises of Theology Concerning Servant-Led
Institutions 178

47 Servant Leadership and Forgiveness 181

48 Servant Leadership: The Movement 184

49 Leader, From, Within Blog: 2016 Year in Review 186

50  Servant Leadership and Employee Empowerment          189

51  The Next right Move                                  193

52  10 Core Competencies of Servant Leadership          195

53  Servant Leadership and kindness                     198

*References*                                            201

*Suggested/Additional Reading*                          203

*Author Biography*                                      205

*Crystal J. Davis*

# FOREWORD

*"It's not about me, but it begins with me."*

When Robert K. Greenleaf wrote his seminal essay, the 'Servant as Leader', he put forward an almost impossible challenge to those choosing to follow that path…

Do those served grow as individuals? Do they, while being served, become healthier, wiser, freer, more autonomous, and more likely to become servants themselves? And, what is the effect of this kind of leadership on the least privileged in society? Would they benefit or at least not be further deprived?

On its surface Greenleaf's *'Best test'* seems totally unattainable. But I would say, why not? Isn't that the point? It challenges us to do better. It causes us to think more broadly than we do in our individual, private universes. It encourages us to embrace the many paradoxes that come with taking the servant-leader's path. And … it's an incredibly noble pursuit, therefore worth pursuing.

The hardened skeptic/cynic may view servant-leadership as something that is 'soft' or something that is for 'humanitarian purposes'. It is anything but that. When committing to embrace servant leadership's paradoxes we shift from an 'either/or' way of thinking (and acting) to a 'both/and' approach. It is working to find solutions that often are not easily addressed by yes/no, black/white, on/off thinking. It is seeing the many shades of gray that exist between polarities. Doing this gives us the chance to explore, discover, and co-create alternative paths.

At the end of the day, of the quarter or fiscal year, the ultimate success of an organization depends on the people who make up that organization. As leader, do you take time to listen deeply to your associates? My wise elders often reminded me that you can learn and connect with others more easily by simply listening. In the crazy fast-paced world we face, slowing down and listening is a powerful way of expressing the caring that comes from 'the leader'.

And why should we care about our colleagues? We are human. We want to do good work. And, research consistently shows that employees who sense that the 'boss' cares for and supports them are happier, more engaged, more productive, and it shows up on the bottom line—no matter if that bottom line is a widget, a repaired appliance, or an educated child.

You may now ask, 'this sounds good, but how do I do that?' You just need to start. Just as developing a new skill takes time and practice, so would this. Mistakes will be made and apologized for, as the process requires constant reflection. Think about the time you learned to ride a bike. Were there scraped knees, wobbly rides, and 'oh crap' moments? Of course, there were. You can't watch a YouTube video to learn how to ride a bike, and you can't read a book or watch a TED talk to become a servant-leader. You can get great ideas and insights from the sharing of others. But again … it requires practice and reflection. Rinse and repeat (as it tells us to do on shampoo bottles!)

There is no recipe, to-do list, or 3-ring binder that will *'make you a servant-leader.'* It comes down to each of us having to figure it out for ourselves. There are many resources to assist in this journey of self-learning. This book is one. Ultimately, it's about practice, reflection, and integration with our own unique style and situation(s). So, rinse and repeat!

Dr. Crystal J. Davis provides many insightful thoughts and reflections that can be helpful to any aspiring servant-leader. Would I expect anyone to read this and think 'okay, I'm a servant-leader now.' Of course not. What she gives us are a variety of approaches and philosophies to consider and *reflect* on. Crystal shares from her own inspiring servant-leadership learning journey. Take this opportunity to look more deeply at yourself. Allow yourself to be challenged by ideas you may have never considered. Ask questions, of yourself and of your colleagues. Take what makes sense (today) and weave it into your own practice. Rinse and repeat. It's a continual journey for the servant-leader.

Mistakes will be made. Successes will be achieved. We learn, adapt, and grow. I mentioned the many paradoxes of servant-leadership. Here's one of my favorites. The more effort we put into knowing ourselves (strengths, talents, abilities, beliefs) the more effective we'll be at leading. It's not *about* me, but it *begins* with me.

Jeffrey P. Miller, Ph.D.
Greenleaf Center for Servant-Leadership
Innovative Leadership Solutions
University of Indianapolis
Creighton University

*Crystal J. Davis*

# ACKNOWLEDGMENTS

The journey to self-publishing a book can be overwhelming.

*To Ms. Tajuana Ross*—You are my saving grace! How would I have gotten here without you? You pushed me beyond my place of frustration and fear. You asked me key questions, as a great coach does, that made me self-reflect. The one question you asked that will stay with me for a long time to come is, "Where will you dominate in 2018?" I wrote that down at the top of a clean page in my journal. I thought about that question, meditated on it, and wrote in my journal. I finally got my answer. I wish to thank you so much for stepping in and helping me to make my dream, this book, a reality. Teamwork is dreamwork! I can't wait for what's up ahead for us!

*To Ms. Shreya Chakraborti* – We have worked on two projects together now, and I appreciate your professional skill as an editor. You are able to take my writing and make it better. More importantly, you have a sense of my message to the world and that, my friend, is priceless! Thank you for your consistent collaboration with me on my books and thoughts about how to make the leadership world a better place!

*To Ms. Nilanjana Dey* – Thank you so much for joining us on this project! I appreciate all of the hard work and consistent communication you provided for how to make this book better! Your expertise is valuable to aspiring authors such as myself!

*To Dr. Julie Conzelmann* – Wow, thank you for our friendship and your professional skills. You are a great mentor! We have worked together on many projects and I suppose we are connected for life! As authors and writers, we have completed books that will shape the next generation of servant-leaders, students and organizations that we are connected to and for this, I am grateful.

*To Ms. Holli Sharp* – Wow, thank you for our friendship and your professional skills. You are an ANGEL sent from Heaven! What would I have done without you? I am grateful, so very grateful to you, my friend…

Crystal J. Davis

*To Mr. Marianus Kerketta & Mr. Purna Chandra Sahoo* – Thank you both for your commitment to this journey and the successful outcome!

# THE BACK STORY

Three years ago, I embarked upon a journey that I had no idea where it would go or with whom I could make a positive difference. I just wanted to write about what I was learning. And I was excited about it. One of my morning affirmations was to "Be a beneficial presence in the world." Little did I know that blogging was a direct manifestation of that daily affirmation. The people who follow my blog motivate me to do what I do.

Servant leadership is a way of life for me. I enjoy helping people and organizations to be the absolute best they can be. My definition of servant leadership drives my blogs and my life. I define servant leadership as:

> *"Servant leadership is a smart leadership approach with a moral and ethical center to lead by serving others. Servant leaders' model behaviors that equip and inspire others toward personal greatness. They see people as humans acknowledging their perspectives as legitimate and meaningful. Servant leadership represents a new consciousness and self-awareness that is necessary for engaging others more authentically."*

I pledge to continue writing. I pledge to get better and learn more. Most of all, I pledge to continue to share this knowledge with people that are on this journey with me. I am always open to your thoughts, ideas, and comments!

Reach out to me at Crystal@cjdconsultingsolutions.com ~Dr. Crystal

*Crystal J. Davis*

# ESSAYS, SEVEN PILLARS OF SERVANT LEADERSHIP: PRACTICING THE WISDOM OF LEADING BY SERVING

by James W. Sipe and Don M. Fri

# 1

## SERVANT LEADERSHIP AND
## CHARACTER (PILLAR I)

*"All leadership development is character development."*

~Stephen Covey[1]

A servant leader is one who makes insightful, moral, and high-principled decisions. More than these, a servant leader:

- is honest, trustworthy, authentic, and humble.
- leads by conscience, not by ego.
- is filled with a depth of awareness, spirit, and enthusiasm.
- is committed to serving something greater than self.

Three of the primary core competencies of a servant-leader are integrity, humility, and service to a higher purpose. How then is character defined? Is it defined by the ability to allow one's conscience-whenever it decides to kick in-to inform one's behavior and move the person to make the necessary decision? Or, is it determined by an individual's flawless record of making right and moral decisions? Well, I would say that we *all* have made mistakes.

Sipe and Frick (2009)[2] highlight a story to illustrate this point. Jane (a pseudonym) worked for a huge global retail and underhandedly used a consultant's detailed project proposal to create her own training initiatives. Jane couldn't sleep at night. She knew she had done something unethical, and this bothered her. In the end, she called the consultant to tell him that he would not get the contract. She did not anticipate his tears. His small consulting firm had made the final list to work with her global retail giant, and he had provided everything she asked for in each call Jane made. He was devastated at the news. Jane thought she could satisfy her conscience by compensating the consultant for his time and efforts. In the end, Jane did not let her conscience be her guide. She even received an enormous bonus from the supervisor who helped her rationalize her actions.

A servant-leader lives, loves, and leads by conscience—the internal moral awareness of what is right and what is wrong. Stephen Covey lamented that conscience is the difference between the leadership that *works* and the leadership that *endures*. Character can be taught and built. As a matter of fact, Joseph Badaracco said that we form our character in defining moments, many in private.[3] Others never witness the effects of private defining moments. But when they do, they become 'moments of truth (MOT).' Many times, a positive MOT results in a purchase, a satisfied customer, repeat business, referrals, and on good will. On the other hand, a negative MOT damages credibility, reduces trust, and compromise's the leader's effectiveness.

As a young leader, I have had many moments of truth to build my character. When I think back, I realize that had I not made some mistakes I would not have been able to build the character I have today. Now instead of looking back with regret, I look back and see how far I've come regarding character building. After all, there are many 'values in action' that form the character of a servant-leader; maintaining integrity, demonstrating humility and service to a higher purpose. Do you have a MOT that helped to define your character? Many leadership writers have suggested that a person of character is one whose compass stays focused on the 'True North.' Bill George, former CEO of Medtronic said,

"True North is the internal compass that guides you successfully through life. It represents who you are as a human being at your deepest level. It is your orienting point-your fixed point in a spinning world-that helps you stay on track as a leader. Your True North is based on what is most important to you, your most cherished values, your passions, and motivation, the sources of satisfaction in your life."[4]

This week contemplate your True North. It will never lead you astray!

*Crystal J. Davis*

Namaste,
Dr. Crystal

## Notes

1. James W. Sipe and Don M. Frick, *Seven Pillars of Servant Leadership: Practicing the Wisdom of Leading by Serving*, (New York Mahwah, NJ: Paulist Press, Inc., 2009) 15.
2. Sipe and Frick, *Seven Pillars*.
3. Joseph Badaracco, Jr., "The Discipline of Building Character," *Harvard Business Review on Leadership, 76*(2) (1998), 114.
4. Bill George, "True North," *Georgia Tech Alumni Magazine* (Fall 2007), 47.
5. http://www.truenorthleaders.com/images/Georgia_tech_bill_george_web.pdf

# 2

# SERVANT LEADERSHIP AND PUTTING PEOPLE FIRST (PILLAR II)

*"The joy of giving is its own reward."*

~Kahil Gibran

Last week, we discussed the first pillar of servant leadership that defined a servant-leader as a person of character. The second pillar of servant leadership, as discussed in James Sipe and Don Frick's book, *Seven Pillars of Servant Leadership*, is that a servant-leader **puts people first**.[2] A leader in service to people makes sure that their highest priorities and developmental needs are met. The characteristics of a servant-leader are such that they:

- seek first to serve, and then aspire to lead.
- show by their actions that their self-interest is deeply connected to the needs and interests of others.
- serve in a manner that allows those served to grow as persons.
- express genuine care and concern for others.

The three core competencies of a servant-leader who puts people first are:

- they display a servant's heart.
- they are mentor-minded.
- they show care and concern.

It has been proven that companies and organizations that put people first, outperform their competitors. Ironically, the practice of putting people before profits, makes an organization or company even *more* profitable. In fact, the Sipe and Frick (2009)[3] revealed data on servant-led companies and their uber financial performance. What they found is that these businesses

4

have servant-leaders who focus on serving rather than helping. When we are serving, we are listening to others; we are concerned with their knowledge, skills, as well as with their emotional and behavioral dynamics. When we are helping others, the emphasis is on what we know about them, and what we can do for them. This is an essential point. Servant-leaders not only help by action but also serve by actions *and* by their simple presence.

Many leaders describe their desire to serve as a 'calling.' To think of it in this way in today's highly-competitive, consumer-based world doesn't mesh well with prevailing acumen, but the impression resides in the heart of the servant-leader. We know in today's shrewd business culture, that the word 'love' is awkward. We are more accustomed to hearing this word in church settings. In this context, we are speaking of love as acting intentionally in ways that support the health, wisdom, freedom, and independence of other people. It's about meeting others' critical needs and not the narrow egotistical needs of self.

Love is the most lasting of all emotions. In this way, love is expressed through a servant-leader's presence amongst others, holding oneself accountable, and putting people first. Love of a servant-leader who is mentor-minded, rejoices in the growth and expansion of others, no matter how different from his own. To conclude, I would say, this is how servants love, and this is how servant-leaders lead.

To leading,
Dr. Crystal

## Notes

1. James W. Sipe and Don M. Frick, *Seven Pillars of Servant Leadership: Practicing the Wisdom of Leading by Serving*, (New York Mahwah, NJ: Paulist Press, Inc., 2009), 34.
2. Sipe and Frick, *Seven Pillars*, 34.
3. Sipe and Frick, *Seven Pillars*, 35.
4. Sipe and Frick, *Seven Pillars*, 44.

# 3

# SERVANT LEADERSHIP AND SKILLED COMMUNICATION (PILLAR III)

*"A true natural servant automatically responds to any problem by listening first."*

~Robert Greenleaf

Last week, we discussed the second pillar of servant leadership, putting people first. The third pillar of servant leadership, as discussed in James Sipe and Don Frick's book, *Seven Pillars of Servant Leadership*, is that a servant-leader is a **skilled communicator**.[2] A servant-leader who is skilled in communication:

- listens earnestly and is an active speaker.
- seeks first to understand and then to be understood.
- is receptively listening to others while demonstrating authentic warmth, respect, and interest.
- is always inwardly mindful of and with self and welcomes feedback from others.
- is influential from a base of assertiveness and persuasion rather than power and position.

The three core competencies of a servant-leader who is a skilled communicator are:

- they demonstrate empathy.
- they invite feedback.
- they communicate persuasively.

6

It is understood that the skilled communicator is one who has high-level people skills. They are the servant-leaders who display empathy (deep, accurate understanding), warmth (kindness and respect), genuineness (authenticity), concreteness (concrete and direct), initiative (solution-oriented and risk-taker), immediacy (here-and-now sharing), appropriate self-disclosure (sharing of self), confrontation (challenging others to grow), and self-exploration (inward self-reflection, and open to feedback).

These types of soft skills are in demand in the 21st century business industry. I posted an article from the *Sydney Morning Herald* in which the author discussed the push from business leaders for the Melbourne Business School in Australia to include soft skills into their business courses.[3] They wanted students (especially high-tech students) to hone in on these skills and build their leadership as well as people skills, such as the ones mentioned above. Be it in relationships, business acumen, or in global insight, it is imperative that leaders today can deliver. Enterprises and companies are looking for leaders and employees who are self-aware and authentic.

The most critical in the list of people skills is, empathy. Being empathetic is being keenly aware of another person's thoughts, feelings, and needs. More than that, it is being able to understand another's experience. The Toro Company in southwest Minnesota knows all too well about empathy.

Ken Melrose, the former CEO of the Toro Company, shared the story of empathy in action.[4] Once, there were complaints that the assembly lines were too slow. The management of the Toro Company was challenged to prove that quality products could be made at a greater speed. Well, you know what happened. The managers ran the lines for a day. They were consistently hitting the buttons to stop the lines, decreasing the line rate by 60%. At the end of the day, the management was in awe at how the 'hourly workers' could keep the line going and engage in small talk about their lives, families, and so on. The management realized that many of the 'hourly workers' lived their everyday life just like they themselves did. Talk about empathy! The Toro Company began to send out corporate and divisional managers to visit and work at the plants. They began to instill a culture of empathy which they still do today.

Carl Rogers, who we know as the father of humanistic psychology, said this about the power of empathy:

'Being fully present means entering the private perceptual world of another and becoming thoroughly at home in it. It involves being sensitive, moment by moment, to the changing felt meanings which flow in this other person, to the fear or rage or tenderness or confusion, or whatever he or she is experiencing. It means temporarily living in the other's life; moving about in it delicately without making judgements. **For empathy, presence must precede practice.**'[5]

The best way to connect in empathy is to listen. Indeed, listening with full presence and attention is *the* premier skill of a servant-leader.

To listening,
Dr. Crystal

## Notes

1. James W. Sipe and Don M. Frick, *Seven Pillars of Servant Leadership: Practicing the Wisdom of Leading by Serving*, (New York Mahwah, NJ: Paulist Press, Inc., 2009), 45.
2. Sipe and Frick, *Seven Pillars*, 45.
3. http://www.smh.com.au/national/the-rise-of-soft-skills-why-top-marks-no-longer-get-the-best-jobs-20150314-1440ds.html
4. Sipe and Frick, *Seven Pillars*, 53.
5. Sipe and Frick, *Seven Pillars*, 55.

## 4

# SERVANT LEADERSHIP AND COMPASSIONATE COLLABORATION (PILLAR IV)

*"None of us is perfect by ourselves..."*

~Robert Greenleaf[1]

A servant-leader builds relationship, embraces diversity, and is the creator of a culture of collaboration. Pillar IV is the servant-leader as **compassionate collaborator.** A servant-leader who compassionately collaborates:

- invites and rewards the contribution of others.
- is always mindful and aware of the quality of work-life balance and continually builds caring, supportive, and collaborative teams and communities.
- develops a positive rapport with diverse people, acknowledges cultural difference, and values a variety of backgrounds.
- neutralizes disagreements respectfully, diplomatically, and constructively.

The three core competencies of a servant-leader who is a compassionate collaborator are that they:

- express appreciation.
- build teams and communities.
- negotiate conflict.

Because servant-leaders know that:

- **T**ogether
- **E**veryone

- **A**chieves
- **M**ore

Servant-leaders develop a culture of collaboration. This type of culture takes time to build, but a servant-leader knows it is the way to harmony (as it is seen in Japanese cultures) and the success of an organization or project. A collaborative culture includes:

- trust and respect in everyday situations,
- equalitarian attitudes among members of all ranks,
- power based on expertise and accountability,
- shared leadership where all members take initiative,
- commitment to the success of other members, rather than to just one's own success,
- valuing truth and honesty
- commitment to continuous improvement of the whole organization,
- active learning, and
- personal responsibility.

Building a culture of collaboration is worth the work. As a servant-leader strives to reach a consensus about doing the right thing, one comes to understand quickly, that the right thing may be different for the customer, the manager, or the boss. To engage in a consensus decision-making, a servant-leader understands that while everyone may not agree with the ultimate decision, everyone is going to support the decision and not undermine it. At the end of the day, the servant-leader could be said to have engaged in compassionate collaboration when everyone who leaves the room would claim that 'we' made the decision and not just the leader.

One of the three competencies of a compassionate collaboration is expressing appreciation. Five tips that servant-leaders engage in when praising people are:

**Praise with a purpose**
Understand the difference between a compliment and a praise that reinforces positive performance. For example, telling Jane you like her new

glasses is a compliment. Telling Jane that you appreciate her contribution in helping the organization stay systematic and efficient is effective praise.

## Be specific
"Good job, way to Go!" is a good way to show appreciation but what's even better is saying, "What an impressive procedure you developed for handling customer service conflicts on the telephone." Be brief and precise.

## Consider the receiver
It helps to be aware of generation-sensitive language (You wouldn't want to say "good job, dude" to a person who is seen as an elder) and of the personality and feelings of the receiver of your recognition. John might prefer a quiet hallway conversation while Sally might appreciate a banner or balloons. Know your people!

## Be sincere
Be genuine, let your praise be heartfelt, and commensurate with the situation. People can sense phoniness and brown-nosing a mile away.

## Do it often
Celebrate small successes—frequently, consistently, and conscientiously. It is good business, and it is one way a servant-leader acts on her commitment to the growth of others.

Crislip and Larson, in their book, *Collaborative Leadership* (2007) said, "The purpose of collaboration is to create a shared vision and joint strategies to address concerns that go beyond the purview of any particular party."[2]

Servant-leaders understand that the growth of self and others is interrelated with compassionate collaboration. Without it, failure is inevitable.

To collaborating,
Dr. Crystal

## Notes

1. James W. Sipe and Don M. Frick, *Seven Pillars of Servant Leadership: Practicing the Wisdom of Leading by Serving,* (New York Mahwah, NJ: Paulist Press, Inc., 2009), 77.
2. Sipe and Frick, *Seven Pillars*, 82.

# 5

# SERVANT LEADERSHIP AND FORESIGHT (PILLAR V)

*"No one is ever as shocked and surprised as when the inevitable occurs."*

~Paul Baran

The fifth pillar of servant leadership as described in James Sipe and Don Frick's book, *Seven Pillars of Servant Leadership*, is about a servant-leader who possesses **foresight**.[2] A servant-leader, who possesses foresight, imagines limitless possibilities, forecasts the future and moves forward with a clear purpose. A servant-leader with foresight has the following characteristics: They;

- view foresight as the central ethic of leadership.
- know how to access the inner intuition.
- articulate and encourage a shared vision.
- see creativity as a strategic tool.
- are discerning, decisive, and courageous decision-makers.

Three core competencies of a servant-leader who possesses foresight are such that they:

- are visionary.
- display creativity.
- take courageous, decisive action.

Robert Greenleaf suggested in his book, *Servant as Leader* (2015) that foresight is, "To [sic] have a sense for the unknowable and be able to foresee the unforeseeable."[3] Possessing foresight is the ability to have people follow you, trust you, and trust your foresight. What struck me very powerfully, is the idea that foresight is deeply aligned with the intuitive mind. I believe that is why we may have challenges with foresight; it asks us to trust our inner guidance as a source of inspiration for leadership and for motivating others.

We have become indoctrinated to follow everything but our own internal compass. As a child, I always felt inclined to obey, believe and listen to everything outside of myself (parents, school, church, family, etc.) even though I had inner thoughts or notions that were different. It wasn't until I was an adult that I dropped the outer for the inner. This is exactly what Robert Greenleaf spoke about. It is essential to our growth as servant-leaders.

Intuition is valuable, but, what is more valuable is the decision to **act** on the impulse of intuition. As servant-leaders, it is of great value to us to trust our hearts and our gut intuitions because they go far beyond the analytical work to evolve and expand the idea of foresight. What we can learn from foresight is that it is indeed different from planning. Daniel Kim (2002) said foresight is, "the significance and nature of events before they occur... to make predictions that can guide followers to a better future."[4]

Daniel Kim's book, *Foresight as the Central Ethic of Leadership* (2002), is a powerful description of foresight, awareness vision, reflective action, mental models, choice, and seeing. I believe Kim's thoughts are summed up in Greenleaf's writings on foresight and on the role of vision:

> "Awareness is not a giver of solace. It is just the opposite. It is the disturber and an awakener. Able leaders are usually sharply awakened and reasonably disturbed. They are not seekers after solace. They have their own inner serenity."[5]

Wow!

Foresight is inextricably tied to the invincible Spirit (God, or whatever name you choose). The inner knowing (intuition) is where the Spirit speaks to us. Meditation helps guide us to that place where if we listen, we can hear the small, still voice of the Spirit. Sipe and Frick (2009) discuss meditation; however, in the book they call it *silence*.[6] This is the best way in which to tap into intuition and to learn to trust its guidance. It is a journey, but a worthwhile one.

Caroline Myss (2004), in her book, *Invisible Acts of Power: Channeling Grace in Your Everyday Life,* says about intuition, "Never, ever underestimate the inherent power that exists within your own archive of wisdom, and never ever judge the quality of your wisdom by the response of the listener."[7]

Early in my leadership career, that statement hit me like a ton of bricks! Seeking validation outside of oneself is dangerous. Moreover, Myss discusses acts of service, which align with servant leadership. She also ties in the godly aspect of our inner life. Myss says:

"Mystics and saints maintain a consciousness of the presence of God within themselves and others. They aim to practice this mindfulness at every moment-at prayer, at work, when dealing with each other. Out of this practice of noticing, of awakening to who is around us and what is around us, out of this mindfulness of ourselves and others, we create invisible acts of power.[8]"

To summarize, Kim gives us the greatest challenge of all in developing foresight. Indeed, it goes hand-in-hand with intuition and leading from foresight:

"The ability to be clear about one's life purpose is critical for establishing a strong foundation on which all future choices will rest. This requires profound self-knowledge and high personal mastery for a leader to be clear about WHO she is, which in turn requires a deep awareness of one's core values that define who we are.[9]"

Kim's book could have just been a sermon for me and to that I say a resounding, "Amen!"

To foresight,
Dr. Crystal

## Notes

1. James W. Sipe and Don M. Frick, *Seven Pillars of Servant Leadership: Practicing the Wisdom of Leading by Serving,* (New York Mahwah, NJ: Paulist Press, Inc., 2009), 104.
2. Sipe and Frick, *Seven Pillars,* 104.
3. Sipe and Frick, *Seven Pillars,* 106.

4. Daniel Kim, *Foresight as the central ethic of leadership*, (Atlanta, GA: The Greenleaf Center for Servant-Leadership, 2002), 3.
5. Kim, *Foresight*, 5.
6. Sipe and Frick, *Seven Pillars*, 7.
7. Caroline Myss, *Invisible acts of power: Channeling grace in your everyday life*, (New York, NY: Atria Paperback, 2004),29
8. Myss, *Invisible acts*, 37.
9. Kim, *Foresight*, 15.

# 6

# SERVANT LEADERSHIP AND SYSTEMS THINKING (PILLAR VI)

*"When you look at anything or consider anything, look at it as "a whole" as much as you can before you swing on it."*

~Robert Greenleaf

James Sipe and Don Frick discuss the seven characteristics of servant leadership in their book, *Seven Pillars of Servant Leadership: Practicing the Wisdom of Leading by Serving*. Since I am a conceptual thinker most of the time (I took the Emergentics personality profile with a group of board members), I jumped straight to the chapter on **systems thinkers**[2]. Servant-leaders who think systemically:

- connect system thinking with ethical issues,
- apply servant leadership to systems analysis and decision making,
- integrate input from all parties in a system to arrive at holistic solutions, and
- demonstrate an awareness of how to lead and manage change.

Servant-leaders use tools such as the Baldridge National Quality Program, Six Sigma, Appreciative Inquiry, Change Management, and a plethora of other tools designed to see things in their entirety and to find the appropriate language to express it. They need to distance themselves from the immediate situation in order to see the problems in the context of the patterns and structures of the entire organization and also, that organization's relationship to its environment, its community and to the country.

System thinkers generally refer to the Systems Pyramid to illustrate the dynamics of systems thinking—events, strategies, culture and beliefs.

**Events** – Are at the top of the pyramid and are considered above ground and in conscious view. These are the situations we see and react to.

**Strategies** – Are below the events and are often created in response to events or to a vision of what should happen.

**Culture** – Can either support or sabotage strategies but is certainly more powerful than strategy. An organization's culture is a mash-up of causal connections, relationships, and a history of patterns that are rigid and have become a part of the policies and assumptions of the organization.

**Beliefs** – Quietly run the **entire** show in organizations. An organization bent on the bottom line only fosters a radically different culture than an organization that runs its enterprise on the belief that it should contribute to the growth of the people and serve the wider public.

Edward Deming said that workers are only responsible for 15% of the problems while the overall system is responsible for the other 85%.[3] For servant-leaders, this is huge. Robert Greenleaf posited four invitations for servant-leaders who wish to think systemically:

- wholeness requires moving in the right direction. If you are certain of the direction, the goal will reveal itself in due course.
- a servant-leader sees life in all its glorious messiness without all the loose ends tied up in neat, simplistic bows. One must learn to live peacefully and sleep well with a submerged awareness of constant danger.
- a servant-leader loves the sheer beauty of this world and everything in it.
  Servant-leaders cultivate a heightened sense of awareness and are able to see the connections between history, people, events, possibilities, and deep intuition.
- a servant-leader deeply understands that ethical conduct is central to seeing things whole. Servant-leaders take personal responsibility and act ethically, doing what can be done with the resources at hand.

Are you willing to stand out as a servant-leader Systems Thinker? If so, we know that you are one who goes out ahead to show the way (the quality of a servant-leader) and uses a well-researched method (Systems Thinking) for moving ahead on the journey.

To leading,
Dr. Crystal

## Notes

[1] James W. Sipe and Don M. Frick, *Seven Pillars of Servant Leadership: Practicing the Wisdom of Leading by Serving,* (New York Mahwah, NJ: Paulist Press, Inc., 2009), 130.
[2] Sipe and Frick, *Seven Pillars,* 130.
[3] Sipe and Frick, *Seven Pillars,* 135.

# 7

# SERVANT LEADERSHIP AND MORAL AUTHORITY (PILLAR VII)

*"Moral authority requires sacrifice."*

~ Stephen Covey

A servant-leader is worthy of respect, inspires trust and confidence, and establishes quality standards for performance. Pillar number seven in James Sipe and Don Frick's book, *Seven Pillars of Servant Leadership*, is **moral authority**.[2] Servant-leaders that exemplify moral authority:

- value moral authority over positional authority,
- empower others with authority as well as with responsibility,
- set clear and firm, yet flexible boundaries.

The three core competencies of a servant-leader with moral authority are such that they:

- accept and delegate responsibility.
- share power and control.
- create a culture of accountability.

Moral authority is quite different from formal authority. The latter is a part of one's official title or position. Moral authority, on the other hand, is not something that comes with position; indeed, it is **earned**. How is it earned? This is done by following the other six pillars of servant leadership.

Your employees, your followers, your family and friends grant you moral authority when they see you consistently:

- act with character, humility, integrity, and a foundation of spirituality,
- put people first through caring and concern, mentoring and selfless service,

- communicate skillfully using empathy and an open heart as guideposts,
- collaborate compassionately, respect diversity, build and empower effective teams, and face conflict head-on,
- trust intuition and use foresight, nurture and value creativity, inspire and support an authentic vision, and,
- think holistically, always considering the greater good and moving strategically in complex and fluid environments and organizations.

Moral authority is more than that of the esteemed leader. It can mean survival or the *demise* of an organization. Parents understand this concept all too well. Parents know that telling children, "Do what I say, not what I do", does not work with kids. Children watch and mimic what their parents do and so child-rearing and leading cannot be done through ego but only through love … love of self and love of others.

Robert Greenleaf, in his book, *Servant Leadership: A Journey into the Nature of Legitimate Power and Greatness* (1977) put it this way,

"A new moral principle is emerging which holds that the only authority deserving our allegiance is that which is freely and knowingly granted by the led to the leader in response to, and in proportion to, the clearly evident servant stature of the leader. Those who choose to follow this principle will not casually accept the authority of existing institutions. Rather, they will freely respond only to individuals who are chosen leader because they are proven and trusted as servants. To the extent that this principle prevails in the future, the only truly viable institutions will be those that are predominantly servant led.[3]"

Whew! Powerful stuff, right? Abraham Lincoln reminds us that actions speak louder than words.[4] As emerging servant-leaders, we understand that moral authority is ultimately a by-product of acting as a servant-leader, not a goal in and of itself. At the end of the day, a servant-leader's moral authority is scored by others. And that's exactly how it should be.

To moral authority,
Dr. Crystal

## Notes

1  James W. Sipe and Don M. Frick, *Seven Pillars of Servant Leadership: Practicing the Wisdom of Leading by Serving*, (New York Mahwah, NJ: Paulist Press, Inc., 2009), 155.
2  Sipe and Frick, *Seven Pillars*, 155.
3  Sipe and Frick, *Seven Pillars*, 157.
4  'Actions speak louder than words' was first used in its current form in the USA by Abraham Lincoln in 1856. https://www.biography.com/people/abraham-lincoln-9382540

## ESSAYS, THE SPEED OF TRUST: THE ONE THING THAT CHANGES EVERYTHING
by Stephen M. R. Covey

*Crystal J. Davis*

# 8

# SERVANT LEADERSHIP AND TRUST

*"Our distrust is very expensive."*

~Ralph Waldo Emerson[1]

Stephen M. R. Covey (Stephen R. Covey's son) defines trust in his book, *The Speed of Trust: The One Thing That Changes Everything* as something that, "You know when you feel it."[2] Trust in relationships is built on confidence. If you have confidence in a person, perhaps in a boss, a co-worker, a family member, or friend, the relationship feels good, there is good communication, you can get tasks done quickly, and you enjoy the relationship.

On the other hand, if you are involved in a low-trust relationship, it may feel as if communication is broken, things are not getting done quickly, there are constant misunderstandings, and the relationship is tedious, cumbersome, and draining. Indeed, there are many differences between high and low-trust relationships.

Organizationally speaking, trust within companies and businesses has declined. Recent research shows:

- only 51% of employees have trust and confidence in management and leadership.
- just about 36% of employees believe their managers, supervisors, and leaders act with honesty and integrity.
- a whopping 76% of employees have witnessed illegal or unethical behavior on the job. Behavior that if exposed, would violate the public trust.

- the number one reason why people leave their jobs is due to a bad relationship with a boss.[3]

What can be done about increasing trust on the job? Cynics often ask if trust can be measured. Can trust be seen as an economic driver? Well, Covey makes the case that it can. Trust affects two outcomes; speed and cost.

This insight says that when trust goes down, speed will also go down, and costs will go up.

$\downarrow$ Trust = $\downarrow$ Speed $\uparrow$ Cost

Conversely, when trust goes up, speed will also go up, and costs will go down.

$\uparrow$ Trust = $\uparrow$ Speed $\downarrow$ Cost

Covey illustrates this through the example of post 9/11 and the new security processes put in place at airports across the country. Clearly, we need the extra security measures to protect our safety. However, it slowed down the process and increased the cost of flying.

Covey goes further to say that trust is a function of *character* and *competence*. Both aspects are important to trust as character involves one's integrity, motives, and intentions while competence includes one's skills, results, track record, and capabilities. Covey makes a serious and noteworthy claim that the side of trust that is a function of character is, "fast becoming the price of entry in the new global economy."[5]

Think about it. People trust people who make things happen.

Leaders give the promising projects or sales leads to those who have performed in the past. Universities give the new curriculum to the most competent instructors. Students who show promising skills get the coveted internships.

Servant-leaders understand the balance between character and competence. These are the foundational building blocks of trust. Through the five waves of trust (Self-Trust, Relationship Trust, Organizational Trust, Market Trust, and Societal Trust), servant-leaders can build stronger, sustainable relationships, provide more opportunities, envision better outcomes, and have fun! What a concept!

Servant-leaders know from a deep well within that trust impacts everything in one's life. The way you lead, establish, grow, restore, and extend help, all depend on one thing. And that my friends, is trust.

To trust,
Dr. Crystal

## Notes

1. S. M. R. Covey, *The speed of trust: The one thing that changes everything*, (New York, NY: Free Press, 2006), 14.
2. Covey, *Speed of Trust*, 5.
3. Covey, *Speed of Trust*, 11-12.
4. Covey, *Speed of Trust*,13.
5. Covey, *Speed of Trust*, 30.

9

# SERVANT LEADERSHIP AND SELF-TRUST

*"Self-trust is the first secret of success…the essence of heroism."*

~Ralph Waldo Emerson[1]

Stephen M. R. Covey (Stephen R. Covey's son) illustrates the 'Five Waves of Trust' model in his book, *The Speed of Trust: The One Thing That Changes Everything.*[2] He uses the metaphor of a wave to demonstrate how trust operates in our professional and personal lives. Trust is important in our relationships, in our organizations and in our world. The trust model presented in this book aligns with servant leadership as it is an *inside-out* approach to harness trust in ourselves and then extend that trust to others. Indeed, servant-leaders know that to be successful, one must lead from within.

Servant-leaders understand that Self-Trust is the foundational principle to building credibility. Covey argues that there are four core elements that help to increase credibility; two of the core elements are related to **competence** and the other two are related to **character**. Let us look at these four core elements in detail.

## The Four Cores
### Core 1: Integrity (of character)
Integrity is related to honesty. While honesty is important, integrity is about consistency or congruency. Being congruent, in balance, with yourself inside and out is a key element of integrity. Congruence is not compliance. Servant-leaders realize that leaders who are congruent act in harmony with their values and beliefs. They walk the walk and talk the talk. There is a synergy that exists, and these leaders listen, operate and respond from a higher level of consciousness. More than that, integrity involves humility. A

humble person is concerned about what is right, rather than being right. They act on good ideas and are not worried about having the first idea; they *recognize* good work rather than *being recognized* for good work. We must not confuse this type of inner consciousness with being weak or reticent. In fact, leading from this place allows servant-leaders to stand firm in principle, negotiate fiercely, drive a good bargain, and express themselves in firm and clear ways. Finally, humble leaders always remember that they stand on the shoulders of those who have gone before them, and they respect and honor this fact.

## Core 2: Intent (of character)

Intent is related to one's plan or purpose. One's intention is directly related to motive, agenda, and behavior. Servant-leaders know that the motive that inspires the greatest trust, is caring. Caring about people, purposes, the quality of your leadership, and caring about the world is paramount. Leaders who care, understand that declaring your intent and expressing your agenda and motives, can be powerful as well as meaningful. This is especially true if your behavior or decisions are being questioned or misrepresented by others. Declaring your intent is important when establishing trust in new relationships.

## Core 3: Capabilities (of competence)

Servant-leaders are capable of establishing, growing, extending, and restoring trust through the way they use their talents, attitudes, skills, knowledge and style. Capabilities are the means by which servant-leaders produce results and perform with excellence. Moreover, capability is vital to one's credibility—both personally and organizationally. Capable people are credible. They inspire trust. It's just that simple. It would be disastrous if a servant-leader had all three of the other core elements and lacked capability.

## Core 4: Results (of competence)

Craig Weatherup, former CEO of Pepsico, said "You can't create a high-trust culture unless people perform."[3] Results are directly tied to a servant-leader's credibility. Results have the ability to help a leader establish and maintain trust. Results bring a type of clout that says you are a producer and a performer. Nothing proves servant leadership better than great results! But we must be careful in pushing for results and forget that integrity is equally important. Leaders who live with values and integrity but achieve low results can be trained, coached, and moved to another role. But, the harder pill to swallow is if a leader produces high results but lives by poor values.

Servant-leaders are clear that employees and followers notice the Four Cores in your daily work and personal life. They understand that credibility is crucial and understanding and living by the Four Cores bring conscious competence that, in the end, enhance trust in the people and in the organization.

To self-trust,

Dr. Crystal

## Notes

1 S. M. R. Covey, *The speed of trust: The one thing that changes everything*, (New York, NY: Free Press, 2006), 46.

2 Covey, *Speed of Trust*, 32.

3 Covey, *Speed of Trust*, 109.

## 10

# SERVANT LEADERSHIP AND RELATIONSHIP TRUST

*"You may be deceived if you trust too much, but you will live in torment if you don't trust enough."*

~Frank Crane, author and columnist[1]

Stephen Covey (Stephen R. Covey's son) highlights the second wave of trust in his book, *The Speed of Trust: The One Thing That Changes Everything* as **relationship trust**.[2] This wave of trust is all about behavior…consistent behavior. Covey provides 13 behaviors that if considered in our daily personal and work lives, would benefit servant-leaders. The principle of behavior is about learning how to interact with others in ways that increase trust and avoid interacting in ways that destroy it.

## The 13 Behaviors
### Behavior 1: Talk straight
Tell the truth and leave the right impression. Be honest. Let people know where you stand. Use simple language. Call things what they are. Demonstrate integrity. Do not manipulate people or distort facts. Do not twist the truth.

### Behavior 2: Demonstrate respect
Genuinely care for others. Show you care. Respect the dignity of every person and every role. Treat everyone with respect, especially those who can't do anything for you. Show kindness in little things. Do not fake caring. Do not attempt to be 'efficient' with people.

**Behavior 3: Create transparency**
Tell the truth in a way people can verify. Get real and genuine. Be open and authentic. Operate on the premise of, 'What you see is what you get.' Do not have hidden agendas. Do not hide information.

**Behavior 4: Right wrongs**
Make things right when you are wrong. Apologize quickly. Make restitution where possible. Practice 'service recoveries.' Demonstrate personal humility. Don't let pride get in the way of doing the right thing.

**Behavior 5: Show loyalty**
Give credit freely. Acknowledge the contributions of others. Speak about people as if they were present. Represent others who aren't there to speak for themselves. Do not bad-mouth others behind their backs. Do not disclose private information of others.

**Behavior 6: Deliver results**
Establish a track record of results. Get the right things done. Make things happen. Accomplish what you have been hired to do. Be on time and within budget. Do not overpromise and under deliver. Do not make excuses for not delivering.

**Behavior 7: Get better**
Continuously improve. Increase your capabilities. Be a constant learner. Develop feedback systems, both formal and informal. Act on the feedback you receive. Thank people for their feedback. Do not assume that today's knowledge will be sufficient for tomorrow's challenges.

**Behavior 8: Confront reality**
Address the tough stuff directly. Acknowledge the unsaid. Lead out courageously in conversation. Remove the 'sword from their hands. 'Do not skirt the real issue. Do not bury your head in the sand.

**Behavior 9: Clarify expectations**

Disclose and reveal expectations. Discuss them. Validate them. Renegotiate them if needed and possible. Do not violate expectations. Do not assume that expectations are clear or shared.

**Behavior 10: Practice accountability**

Hold yourself accountable. Hold others accountable. Take responsibility for results. Be clear on how you shall communicate how you are doing, and how others are doing. Do not avoid or shirk responsibility. Do not blame others or point fingers when things go wrong.

**Behavior 11: Listen first**

Listen before you speak. Understand. Diagnose. Listen not only with your ears—but also with your eyes and your heart. Find out what the most important behaviors are to the people you are working with. Do not assume you know what matters most to others. Do not presume you have all the answers, or all the questions.

**Behavior 12: Keep commitments**

Say what you are going to do, then do what you say you are going to do. Make commitments carefully and keep them. Make keeping commitments the symbol of your honor. Do not break confidences. Do not attempt to 'PR' your way out of a commitment you have broken.

**Behavior 13: Extend trust**

Demonstrate a propensity to trust. Extend trust abundantly to those who have earned your trust. Extend conditionally to those who are earning your trust. Learn how to appropriately extend trust to others based on the situation, risk, and credibility (character and competence) of the people involved. But have a propensity to trust. Do not withhold trust because there is risk involved.

Servant-leaders know that striving daily to expand and grow on each of these behaviors-consistently-is what matters. One's behavior has to become consistent with one's values and relationships. It is the only way to trust.

To relationship trust,
Dr. Crystal

## Notes

[1] S. M. R. Covey, *The speed of trust: The one thing that changes everything*, (New York, NY: Free Press, 2006), 293.

[2] Covey, *Speed of Trust*, 124.

# 11

## SERVANT LEADERSHIP AND ORGANIZATIONAL TRUST

*"Organizations are no longer built on force, but on trust."*

~Peter Drucker[1]

Stephen Covey (Stephen R. Covey's son) highlights the third wave of trust in his book, *The Speed of Trust: The One Thing That Changes Everything* as organizational trust.[2] This wave of trust is all about establishing trust with the internal stakeholders of your organization. We have already discussed the Four Cores of Credibility and the 13 Behaviors.

The third wave of trust lays the foundation for your organization to create value, to establish and maintain trust, to increase speed of product or service delivery, to lower organizational costs, to increase the bottom line, and to maximize influence-yours and that of your organization. The core concept of this wave of trust is considered the **principle of alignment.**

The chapter begins by asking two main questions and gives an illustration of the difference between low-trust and high-trust organizations. The two questions help to gauge how you might apply the above tools to your organization. The two questions are:

- How would you describe a low-trust organization?
- How would you describe a high-trust organization?

The lists consist of the answers Covey's workshop participants provided for both questions. See if you can find your organization in one of these two lists.

**Low-Trust Organizations**

- People manipulate or distort facts
- People withhold and hoard information
- Getting credit is of vital importance
- People spin the truth to their advantage
- New ideas are openly resisted and stifled
- Mistakes are covered up or covered over
- Most people are involved in blame game or in bad-mouthing others
- There is an abundance of gossip
- There are numerous 'meetings after meetings'
- There are many 'undiscussables'
- People tend to overpromise and under deliver
- Energy and consciousness are extremely low
- There are a lot of expectations, for which people try to make excuses
- People pretend bad things are not happening or are in denial
- People often feel unproductive tension, sometimes even fear

Covey's participants who discussed high-trust organizations said they typically saw different behaviors such as:

**High-Trust Organizations**

- Information is shared openly
- Mistakes are tolerated and encouraged as a way of learning
- The culture is innovative and creative
- People are loyal to those who are absent
- People talk straight and confront real issues
- There is real communication and authentic collaboration
- People share credit abundantly
- There are few 'meetings after meetings'
- Transparency is a practical value
- People are candid and authentic

- There is a high degree of accountability
- There exists palpable vitality and energy, a consciousness of positive momentum.[3]

Covey presents four ideas to increase the **principle of alignment** within your organization. Servant-leaders know that integrity, intent, capabilities, and results will yield long-lasting success within the organization. The Four Cores, applied organizationally, can improve trust. This can be seen in the following examples:

**Organizational integrity**

Improve your organization's mission or the statement of its values. Create a culture of keeping commitments-especially in small things. Remember, they are watching how you keep your commitments.

**Organizational intent**

Make sure that your mission and values are reflected in the motives and principles that build trust. Set an example and demonstrate care and concern for everyone. Use systems such as stewardship accountability, rewarding cooperation, and building trust that focus on benefitting everyone on a daily basis.

**Organizational capabilities**

Put systems that attract and retain the talent needed to be competitive in today's global market, in place. Provide on-going professional development, mentoring, and training to promote satisfaction that comes from growth and expansion for the stakeholders. Information and decision-making systems should include everyone to meet organizational goals and customer needs.

**Organizational results**

Create a shared vision for everyone to embrace. Get and keep everyone on the same page. Provide accountability systems for internal stakeholders to get results on a consistent basis. Use balanced scorecards or other systems that meet the needs of the stakeholders, and not just the bosses.

Servant-leaders understand that organizations are severely taxed when low-trust is rampant. And, on the other hand, organizations receive *dividends* when there is high-trust within the organization. The seven taxes for low-trust organizations, along with the seven dividends for high-trust organizations are highlighted below:

**The Seven Low-Trust Organizational Taxes**

- redundancy
- bureaucracy
- politics
- disengagement
- turnover
- churn (turnover other than employees, such as customers, suppliers, distributors, investors, etc.)
- fraud

**The Seven High-Trust Organizational Dividends**

- value
- accelerated growth
- enhanced innovation
- improved collaboration
- stronger partnering
- better execution
- heightened loyalty

I love how Covey brings this chapter to an end by discussing these same core concepts as it relates to family. Everything in this chapter applies just as powerfully to the family as it does to any other organization. For instance, does your family have **integrity**? Are values and guidelines clear? Does our family have good **intent**? Are we kind and caring to one another? What are our family's **capabilities**? Is it safe to learn from mistakes? And finally, what **results** does our family produce? Are systems and processes in place to create joy and share in accomplishments?

Indeed, as servant-leaders in our homes and our workplace modeling the Four Cores and 13 Behaviors, we create an alignment that supports our structure and values. And in doing so, servant-leaders positively affect everything else in our families as well as in our organizations.

To organizational trust,
Dr. Crystal

## Notes

1  S. M. R. Covey, *The speed of trust: The one thing that changes everything*, (New York, NY: Free Press, 2006), 236.
2  Covey, *Speed of Trust*, 236.
3  Covey, *Speed of Trust*, 237

# 12

# SERVANT LEADERSHIP AND MARKET TRUST

*"In the end, all you have is your reputation."*

~Oprah Winfrey[1]

Stephen Covey (Stephen R. Covey's son) highlights the fourth wave of trust in his book, *The Speed of Trust: The One Thing That Changes Everything* as **Market Trust**.[2] This wave of trust is all about brand and reputation. And market trust is about the external stakeholders.

Market Trust is really about the feeling you have that makes you want to buy products or services. It is about investing your time and money and recommending that your friends do the same. A brand is 'trust monetized.'

As a result, companies spend tons of money in creating a brand that inspires people to trust them, their products, and their services.

If you want to improve your brand, Covey argues that your company or organization must strengthen its Four Cores and 13 Behaviors so that you can measurably increase the value of your organization's brand.

Building credibility and trust are key values to servant-leaders and to the marketplace in which they serve.

Considering the perspective of your customers, ask yourself:

1. Does my brand have **integrity?** Do we have a reputation for honesty?
2. Does my brand demonstrate good **intent?** Do people feel that we genuinely care or that we are simply out to 'make a profit?'
3. Does my brand demonstrate **capabilities?** Do people associate our name with quality, excellence, continuous improvement, and relevance?

4. Is my brand associated with **results?** Do people feel we deliver what we promise? Is a good track record associated with our name? Would you recommend us to a friend?

Building one's brand requires that servant-leaders apply the 13 Behaviors and apply those behaviors to external stakeholders, that is, customers, suppliers, distributors, investors, and communities. There are three concepts to consider:

**Talk straight**
Treat customers as if they are educated adults.

**Create transparency**
Create a dynamic self-regulating economy where customers feel the transparency of your organization.

**Listen first**
Genuine listening is one of the truest forms of competitive advantage. Create customer panels. Conduct formal market research, make personal calls to customers, and create loyalty programs. Your customers feel good when they are heard.

Servant-leaders understand that the same concepts that apply at the level of Market Trust also applies to Self-Trust, Relationship Trust, and Organizational Trust.

At the end of the day, whatever trust we are able to create in our organization and in the marketplace, is only the result of the credibility and trust we create in and for ourselves.

To market trust,
Dr. Crystal

## Notes

[1] S. M. R. Covey, *The speed of trust: The one thing that changes everything*, (New York, NY: Free Press, 2006), 261.

2 Covey, *Speed of Trust*, 261.
3 Covey, *Speed of Trust*, 237

# 13

# SERVANT LEADERSHIP AND SOCIETAL TRUST

*"Executives tempted to take shortcuts should remember the dictum of Confucius that good government needs weapons, food, and trust. If the ruler cannot hold onto all three, he should give up weapons first and food next. Trust should be guarded to the end, because without trust, we cannot stand."*

~*Financial Times Editorial*[1]

Stephen Covey (Stephen R. Covey's son) highlights the fifth and final wave of trust in his book, *The Speed of Trust: The One Thing That Changes Everything* as **Societal Trust**.[2] This wave of trust is all about social responsibility. And societal trust creates clearly observable and measurable results.

The overriding principle of Societal Trust is contribution. The intent of contribution is to create harmony, not destroy it and to give back rather than to take. Servant-leaders understand the principle of giving instead of taking. Contribution is aligned with corporate citizenship. Many companies today are involved in corporate citizenship also known as corporate social responsibility. And this makes for a healthy society.

The French proverb, 'fish discover water last', is a great illustration of Societal Trust.[3] For fish, water simply *is*, right? They do not fret or worry about it. They are deeply immersed in it and are unaware of its existence, until it becomes polluted or even non-existent.

In the same way, people discover trust last. That is, they forget that it is an integral part of the fabric of society, until it becomes polluted or compromised. Then the realization hits us that trust is necessary to our very well-being like water is to a fish. Servant-leaders understand that without trust, our society shuts down, and self-destruction is imminent.

Thomas Friedman talks about this in his book, *The World is Flat* (2005), wherein he says that trust is essential to a flat or open society.[4] Flat or open world communities thrive on behaviors such as the 13 Behaviors discussed in Covey's book. To summarize those behaviors again, I ask you, do we as a society:

- talk straight?
- demonstrate respect?
- create transparency?
- right wrongs?
- show loyalty?
- deliver results?
- get better?
- confront reality?
- clarify expectations?
- practice accountability?
- listen first?
- keep commitments?
- extendtrust?[5]

Servant-leaders know that the 13 Behaviors are important on an individual as well as on a societal level. Even more so, the dividends of a **high-trust** society include:

- shared knowledge,
- medical breakthroughs,
- technological advances,
- economic partnerships,
- cultural exchanges, and
- more options and opportunities.[6]

With these ideas in mind, the value of Societal Trust lies in the very fact that servant-leaders commit to a measure of success that takes into account not only the financials of an organization, but also the social and environmental impact. I leave you with a quote from James Surowiecki of *Forbes* magazine on Societal Trust:

"The evolution of capitalism has been in the direction of more trust and transparency, and less self-serving behavior; not coincidentally, this evolution has brought with it greater productivity and economic growth. That evolution, of course, has not taken place because capitalists are naturally good people. Instead, it's taken place because the benefits of trust- that is, of being trusting and of being trustworthy- are potentially immense and because a successful market system teaches people to recognize those benefits."[7]

To societal trust,
Dr. Crystal

## Notes

1  S. M. R. Covey, *The speed of trust: The one thing that changes everything*, (New York, NY: Free Press, 2006), 272.
2  Covey, *Speed of Trust*, 272.
3  Covey, *Speed of Trust*, 273.
4  Covey, *Speed of Trust*, 274.
5  Covey, *Speed of Trust*, 282.
6  Covey, *Speed of Trust*, 274.
7  Covey, *Speed of Trust*, 279

## 14

## SERVANT LEADERSHIP AND GLOBAL CITIZENSHIP

*"The success of big business and the well-being of the world have never been more closely linked. Global issues cannot be removed from the business world because business has only one world in which to operate. Businesses cannot succeed in societies that fail."*

~Jorma Ollila, Chairman and CEO, Nokia[1]

Stephen Covey (Stephen R. Covey's son) reviews the idea of **global citizenship** in his book, *The Speed of Trust: The One Thing That Changes Everything.*[2]

Servant-leaders understand that global citizenship is an individual choice and that it is about you and me making a **conscious** decision to value and always to consider the well-being of others.

Global Citizenship is about caring for others in every dimension of our lives. Covey mentions Gandhi's well-known quote, "One man cannot do right in one department of life whilst he is occupied in doing wrong in another department."[3]

Indeed, life is one indivisible whole. It is inconsistent to provide great customer service while at work and then to ignore the homeless person or neighbor in need who lives on your block.

In doing so, unfortunately, we compartmentalize our lives, and this ultimately makes us feel fragmented and feel like we are living meaningless lives.

When we look at the Four Cores from three perspectives, we can ponder on the following questions as it relates to our self, to our family, and to our organizations:

## Self

1. Am I credible?
2. Do I have intent to do good?
3. Do I contribute to the world selflessly?
4. Am I a person whom society can trust?

## Family

1. Do I exercise the leadership in my family that inspires and helps family members to become good global citizens?
2. Do I set the example?
3. Am I a good citizen within my own family as well as in the world?
4. Do I align family structures and systems in a way that supports citizenship in the family and in the world?
5. Am I teaching my children global citizenship?

## Organizationally

1. Is our organization credible?
2. Do we have integrity, and do we model that behavior?
3. Do we demonstrate intent to do good?
4. Do we have the capabilities to make a difference?
5. Do we produce results for shareholders and stakeholders?
6. Do we give to society an organization they can trust?
7. Does my leadership inspire others to become global citizens?
8. Do we promote citizenship within the organization and also in the world?[4]

For sure, servant-leaders realize that from the first wave (Self-Trust) trust to the fifth wave (Societal Trust), trust flows outward in our relationships, in our organizations, and into the greater world community.

There are four essential themes that emerge from Covey's book. Servant-leaders are smart when they decide to incorporate them into daily living.

**A summary**

1. The Four Cores and 13 Behaviors are the tools that will create and restore trust on every level (the Five Waves of Trust).

2. The main principles of Organizational Trust are **alignment**. That is, making sure that systemic structures and processes within the organizations align with the Four Cores and 13 Behaviors. This builds trust with the internal stakeholders.

3. The main principles of establishing Market Trust is **reputation** or **brand**. The Four Cores and 13 Behaviors inspire trust with external stakeholders to the extent that they will invest, recommend, and/or buy your products and services.

4. The main principles of establishing Societal Trust is **contribution**. This principle is about the intent to give back and to become responsible global citizens.

These concepts are easy to digest intellectually. However, they are a little more challenging in real-world situations. Servant-leaders must look for ways to apply these concepts on an experiential level and to teach them at work and at home.

Not only will servant-leaders better understand and realize the power of the Four Cores and 13 Behaviors, but we will be amazed at the results when you operate at the speed of trust.

To global citizenship,
Dr. Crystal

## Notes

[1] S. M. R. Covey, *The speed of trust: The one thing that changes everything,* (New York, NY: Free Press, 2006), 282.Also from the notes in the back of the book, Jorma Ollila quote: Nokia, "Corporate Responsibility Report," 2004, p. 4. – more information about the book is required.

[2] Covey, *Speed of Trust,* 281.

[3] Covey, *Speed of Trust,* 281.

# 15

# SERVANT LEADERSHIP AND INSPIRING TRUST

*"The first thing for any leader is to inspire trust."*

~Doug Conant, CEO, Campbell Soup Company[1]

As we are nearing the end of our series on trust following Covey's book, *The Speed of Trust: The One Thing That Changes Everything*, we have three final concepts to discuss; extending smart trust, restoring trust when it has been lost, and a propensity to trust.[2]

How difficult is it to **inspire** trust? What servant-leaders understand about trust is that:

1. Nothing can be as profitable as the financial success of trust in the workplace.
2. Nothing is as relevant as the consciousness and the impact of trust.
3. Nothing is as important and valuable to every relationship at every level in your life as the dividends of trust.

But…

Servant-leaders are human, and as such, some residual feelings of fear, hesitancy, and skepticism may block extending trust to others. Somewhere deep in our consciousness we may believe that people can't be trusted, or maybe we grew up or currently work in a low-trust environment.

Even worse, maybe we have been burned in the past. Our trust may have been betrayed. Maybe people had not extended meaningful trust to us.

In this last section of the book, Covey presents us with ideas and concepts about ways in which we can extend what he calls, 'Smart trust.'

The consciousness of smart trust allows servant-leaders to develop skills and competencies that help to avoid the pitfalls and ensures the greatest rewards for everyone.

Servant-leaders can learn to restore trust where it has been lost, and most of all, servant-leaders must develop the propensity to trust. Indeed, it is critical to effective leadership and living.

Finally, servant-leaders understand that extending trust to others is the most important key to developing and sustaining high-trust environments at work and home.

As a matter of fact, 'Extend trust' is one of the 13 Behaviors we have been discussing so far.

At the end of the day, servant-leaders know that their first job is to inspire. Inspiring others is the line in the sand that differentiates the servant-leader from the manager.

To inspire trust is paramount to true and authentic success. As Napoleon Hill said, 'To be inspired is great, to inspire is incredible.'

To inspiring trust,
Dr. Crystal

## Notes

[1] S. M. R. Covey, *The speed of trust: The one thing that changes everything*, (New York, NY: Free Press, 2006), 298.

[2] Covey, *Speed of Trust*, 287, 300, 316.

# 16

# SERVANT LEADERSHIP AND EXTENDING SMART TRUST

*"You may be deceived if you trust too much, but you will live in torment if you don't trust enough."*

~Frank Crane, author and columnist[1]

The last three concepts in Covey's book, *The Speed of Trust: The One Thing That Changes Everything*, are extending smart trust, restoring trust when it has been lost, and a propensity to trust. Today, we look at **extending smart trust.**[2]

Servant-leaders know that when dealing with trust, the perception is that there are two extremes. On the one hand, when you don't trust, four things are happening;

1. You don't trust people enough.
2. You are suspicious of people.
3. You hold things close to your heart.
4. You only trust yourself.

On the other hand, when you trust too much, five things are happening:

1. You are too trusting.
2. You are gullible.
3. You believe anyone and trust everyone.
4. You have a simplistic, naïve view of the world
5. You do not even really think (except superficially) about protecting your interests.

So how do servant-leaders hit the 'sweet spot' in the middle whereby you can extend smart trust to maximize success and minimize risks?[3]

Life is full of risks. The key is not to avoid risk; rather it is to manage risk effectively. That being said, there are two factors to consider when extending smart trust; the propensity to trust and analysis.

## The propensity to trust

This factor is a matter of the heart. It is the wherewithal to believe that people are worthy of trust and that you can extend trust freely. Of course, this predisposition to trust is directly proportionate to your personality, to the way people in your life have trusted you (or not), and to your own experiences—good and bad— in extending trust to others.

## Analysis

This factor is a matter of the mind. It is your ability to analyze, evaluate, and consider the implications and possibilities, and to arrive at sound decisions and positive solutions. This predisposition considers your natural gifts and abilities, your education and your worldview (the way you think), your style, and your life experiences.

In the end, servant-leaders understand the propensity to trust, and analysis gives one the ability to grow, expand, extend, and restore trust. Indeed, this is the key professional and personal competency of servant-leaders. And extending smart trust is a critical part of this competency.

It enables servant-leaders the ability to create a powerful balance and synergy between the two factors—the propensity to trust and analyze, which then enables servant-leaders to effectively leverage self and to inspire in others great talent, unlimited creativity, their highest contribution to the greater world community.

To extending smart trust,
Dr. Crystal

## Notes

[1]  S. M. R. Covey, The speed of trust: The one thing that changes everything, (New York, NY: Free Press, 2006), 293.
[2]  Covey, Speed of Trust, 287.
[3]  Covey, Speed of Trust, 288.
[4]  Covey, Speed of Trust, 281.

17

# SERVANT LEADERSHIP AND RESTORING TRUST

*"I have found that by trusting people until they prove themselves unworthy of that trust, a lot more happens."*

~Jim Burke, former CEO, Johnson & Johnson[1]

The last three concepts in Covey's book, *The Speed of Trust: The One Thing That Changes Everything*, are extending smart trust, restoring trust when it has been lost, and a propensity to trust. Today, we review the second to last concept, **restoring trust when it has been lost.**[2]

We all have been burned. Maybe someone has broken your trust, and you vowed *never* to trust that person again or worse that you will never trust *anyone* again. Maybe you have even tried to restore trust in a person, and it has *failed*. Indeed, maybe there are situations in which trust can never be restored.

However, in life, at some point, we have all made mistakes. We have ruined a professional or personal relationship. A family has been torn apart, or we have made an honest mistake of having failed only to discover that our failure is being interpreted as a violation of character. Friedrich Nietzsche put it best when he said, "There are no facts, only interpretations."[3]

Servant-leaders understand that the idea that trust cannot be restored is a myth; however difficult, trust can be restored and often even enhanced.

The key is that the opportunity to restore trust must be actively sought after to establish it, grow it, restore it, and wisely extend it.

No matter how trust has been compromised, the path leading back to it, is the same; servant-leaders must restore their personal credibility and engage in behavior that inspires trust.

When we look at the Five Waves of Trust that Covey has discussed in the book, we can see how trust can be restored at every level.

## Societal trust
Restoring trust on a societal level means that trust must be built in industries, institutions, organizations, businesses, and in countries. Suspicion and cynicism must be replaced with contribution, value creation, and ethically sound behavior.

## Market trust
It is true that within the global market if trust is lost with a customer, nine times out of ten, that customer will never come back. But, using the Four Cores and 13 Behaviors, integrity makes it possible to restore and enhance trust. It is about service recovery, whereby the problem itself becomes the gateway to create even greater trust. Transparency is an essential tool to restoring market trust.

## Organizational trust
When trust is broken within organizations, one of the most important considerations is to right wrongs and apologize. In this way high-trust organizations continue to perform better than low-trust organizations because employees' value sincere apologies from their leaders.

## Relationship trust
In families and personal relationships, when trust has to be restored, one must be willing and be able to ask for forgiveness. They must then change their behavior and build integrity through character. Family relationships are far more significant and as such one's willingness and openness to restoring trust is greater. In a close personal relationship, the very effort of restoring trust can make the relationship stronger than that it was before.

## Self-trust
The biggest trust of all! It is probably the most difficult trust to restore. When we make promises to ourselves (i.e. I am going to exercise more),

and we violate that trust, we often beat ourselves up badly and our self-worth and self-value take a plunge. We begin to wonder whether we can ever have faith in what we tell ourselves-whether we can trust ourselves. Lack of self-trust undermines our self-confidence and makes us feel unworthy. To restore self-trust, one must review and articulate the 13 Behaviors in one's life. Here is a recap of the 13 Behaviors for self-trust:

1. *Talk straight to yourself.* Do not tell yourself lies such as "I'm worthless, I've blown it."[4] Do not justify bad behavior. Tell yourself the truth and do what you need to do to improve.
2. *Demonstrate respect for yourself.* Treat yourself with as much respect as you would someone else. Do not beat yourself up and demand more of yourself than you would of others.
3. *Create transparency in your life.* Be open and honest with yourself about where you are today and work on being a little better tomorrow.
4. *Right wrongs.* The wrongs you have done to yourself are forgivable. Forgive yourself and free yourself to work on developing self-trust and confidence again.
5. *Show loyalty to yourself.* Do not talk bad about yourself, in your head, or with others. Stop putting yourself down.
6. *Deliver results.* There are goals and ideas in your life that are important to you, no matter what others may feel or think. Set goals and work to accomplish them.
7. *Get better.* Challenge yourself to develop skills and competencies. Seek new knowledge and constantly set aside time to develop your capabilities.
8. *Confront reality.* Do not live in denial and keep your head buried in the sand. Face what you need to face and move forward with confidence.
9. *Clarify expectations.* Be clear with yourself about what you expect and do not let others' expectations rule your life. It is *your* life. Live it with clarity and joy.
10. *Practice accountability.* Follow your own inspiration. If you have an insight, intuition, or idea about your life, follow it and do not allow the expectations of others to control your life.

11. *Listen first.* Take time to listen to your still smaller voice follow your inner guidance. Do not be persuaded by the opinions of others. Do what you are guided to do from within.
12. *Keep commitments.* Make commitments to yourself and respect them as you would your commitments to other people.
13. *Extend trust to yourself.* Trust your inner guidance and instincts. No one has ever said that their instincts have led them down the wrong path. Trust yourself to receive guidance for your life. Trust your heart and *know* that it is right. Everything will always work together for your good!

Phew!!! Good stuff, right?

As I am writing and doing a recap of the 13 Behaviors this morning, I realize that as an *emerging* and *evolving* servant-leader, I have to revisit the 13 Behaviors and hold myself accountable to them.

Once I said to one of my teachers, "How do I teach this stuff when I am still a work in progress? It sometimes feels hypocritical." She said to me, "Crystal, you don't have to be perfect in that which you teach. In fact, you can only teach that which you are learning." If we do not honor ourselves, how can we expect others to?

The 13 Behaviors are a clear and honorable path to strengthen the Four Cores. You remember them, don't you? You will increase your integrity, increase your intent, increase your capabilities, and improve results. It feels good to my soul to know that I can reflect on these each day and get better. And better, and better. In this way, I can become the servant-leader whom *I* can trust, and in turn whom *others* would trust as well.

I have provided us with some heavy stuff today. So, rather than finish the chapter, I will rest here and let us contemplate on these ideas. Next week, I will conclude the thoughts in this chapter before we move ahead to the last concept that Covey talks about, the propensity to trust.

At the end of the day, I have gained much insight and awareness around the Four Cores and 13 Behaviors. I hope that you have, too. These ideas can provide servant-leaders powerful and authentic tools for restoring trust when it has been lost.

To restoring trust,
Dr. Crystal

## Notes

[1] S. M. R. Covey, The speed of trust: The one thing that changes everything, (New York, NY: Free Press, 2006), 316.
[2] Covey, Speed of Trust, 300.
[3] Covey, Speed of Trust, 132.
[4] Covey, Speed of Trust, 310.

# 18

# TO TRUSTING AGAIN

*"The weak can never forgive. Forgiveness is the attribute of the strong."*

~Mahatma Gandhi[1]

Servant-leaders understand that when someone has broken your trust, it is a challenge to forgive and move forward. Covey's book, The Speed of Trust: The One Thing That Changes Everything, in the chapter on **Restoring Trust When it has Been Lost,** provides us with two guidelines to consider when others have lost your trust.[2]

### Do not be too quick to judge

You know what it feels like when you are not trusted. Even worse is when, you have been misunderstood, misinterpreted, or misjudged. Do not assume that a failure of competence equals a failure of character. When we realize that some mistakes are not intentional, we can try not to make something more than it should be.

### Do be quick to forgive

Forgiveness and trust are two different things. We cannot keep forgiving behavior that keeps happening over and over again. This is not smart trust. Forgiveness means that we can heal ourselves from the anger, blaming, vindictiveness, accusing, and retribution toward the person who caused the offense. Whether they did it intentionally or accidentally, we can refuse to take the role of judging them. We can let go of what is not in our control.

Now, forgiveness is not easy and for most of us takes divine intervention. But, whether or not we choose to trust, we must forgive—for our sake and for the sake of others. Until we do, it is difficult for us to exercise s*mart trust*, our a*nalysis*, and our p*ropensity to trust*.

Covey says that "Forgiveness is a principle for a better life. It's about righting wrongs. If we don't forgive, we get in the way of our own clear judgment, emotional freedom, and we may also get in the way of someone else's self-forgiveness and personal change."[3]

This is a pretty heavy concept, right? We get in the way of someone else's self-forgiveness...

Lord Herbert, British philosopher and theologian puts it this way, "He that cannot forgive others breaks the bridge over which he, too, must pass."[4]

Servant-leaders understand that it is in our best interest and the best interest of others to forgive. We are global citizens, a part of the human race, and as such, we can move ahead in resilience knowing that forgiveness brings an inner calm and ever-abiding peace.

For many of us, broken trust is a deal breaker, a dead end. It is the end of a relationship, and even worse, the end of self-confidence in the ability to ever trust again.

**But...**

It does not have to be. It can be the start of a new beginning. Take for example:

**If you have broken trust,**

1. It's an opportunity for you to hit the reset button and begin again.
2. You can improve upon integrity, character, and competence.
3. Adjust your behavior in ways that inspire trust.
4. It provides an opportunity for you to create relationships of high trust going forward.

**If someone has broken trust with you,**

1. increase your own capacity to forgive.
2. extend smart trust.
3. you can maximize the remaining goodness left in the relationship.

In the end, servant-leaders understand that in either situation, broken trust presents an opportunity for one to build up their self-trust and personal credibility. It gives servant-leaders a chance to grow in character and competence. This provides the foundation for increased self-confidence in one's discernment and for his ability to grow, restore, and extend trust at every level of life.

As I write to you this morning, I have been presented with a real-life situation in which I need to put these core values into personal action. I know that when one writes and teaches others about the concepts we've discussed over the past several weeks, I will be called to the carpet on them. It's proof of what my mentor said to me, *"Crystal, you don't have to be perfect in that which you teach. In fact, you can only teach that which you are learning."*

To trusting again,
Dr. Crystal

## Notes

[1]  S. M. R. Covey, The speed of trust: The one thing that changes everything, (New York, NY: Free Press, 2006), 313.
[2]  Covey, Speed of Trust, 300.
[3]  Covey, Speed of Trust, 313.
[4]  Covey, Speed of Trust, 313.

# 19

# PROPENSITY TO TRUST

*"I bring you the gift of these four words; I believe in you."*

~Blaise Pascal, French physicist and mathematician[1]

This blog post will conclude our series on trust and on the book, *The Speed of Trust: The One Thing That Changes Everything*. I am excited about our next series on *compassion*. For this series, we will use the book, *A Force for Good: The Dalai Lama's Vision for Our World* by Daniel Goleman. I have already started reading and boy is there some great stuff up ahead for us as servant-leaders! As always, I so appreciate your support and for following my blogs. I am grateful! I am going to take a week's break to get a jump start on our series! I trust I will see you again soon…

Servant leaders understand that these four words are the most powerful on the planet: *"I believe in you."* Covey's book, *The Speed of Trust: The One Thing That Changes Everything*, reveals the idea about trust in the last chapter, **A Propensity to Trust.**[2]

Have you ever had someone who believed in you wholeheartedly? Especially when no one else did? How did that make you feel?

Servant-leaders understand that someone's faith in you pays off, for them in whatever way that happens, but also for the way their belief in you shapes the trajectory of your life. People's trust in you brings out the best-in you-and in them.

**What does someone's belief and trust in you mean? It means:**

1. we can help them rise to the challenge.
2. we can help them to discover their unseen potential.
3. we can make contributions that benefit us all.

"Even an overdose of trust that, at times, involves the risk of being deceived or disappointed, is wiser in the long run, than taking for granted that most people are incompetent or insincere."[3]

Servant-leaders who extend the propensity to trust become models, mentors, and heroes. We are in a debt of gratitude when we think about how their trust has shaped our lives. Organizationally speaking, companies that choose to extend trust make for great places to work in.

The same is true for the propensity to trust at *home*. Think about the difference parents make when they tell their children, "I love you. I believe in you, I trust you." [4] Indeed, our first job as Servant-leaders is to inspire trust-at work and at home.

## When servant-leaders extend the propensity to trust, here's what happens:

1. Trust brings out the best in people.
2. Trust changes the dynamics of interaction.
3. People live up to the trust that is bestowed upon them.
4. People want to return the trust bestowed upon them.
5. People run by the power of the trust they have been extended.

People respond well to trust and no matter who we are, we have unlimited opportunities to extend and inspire trust. Because, trust, you see, is reciprocal. The more you trust others, the more you, yourself are trusted in return. Lao Tzu puts it this way, "No trust given, no trust received."[5]

The truth is that we were born with the propensity to trust. Think about it. As children, we were innocent, we are vulnerable, and we are gullible. It was not until and through life experience, that we began to trust less and less.

As an *emerging* servant-leader, I have been on both sides of the coin. I have been in leadership positions where I was micromanaged, and trust was not extended. I realized the powerful negative effect on my consciousness, my creativity, my engagement, my excitement, my commitment, and my energy and talent.

On the other hand, I've been in leadership positions where trust was extended, and I know that the trust dramatically inspired and powerfully released the absolute best inside me. Like all of us, I have been burned. But for the most part, I've seen incredible results when people engage in the propensity to trust.

In the end, trust is essential to prosperity, satisfaction, and joy. We can grow it. Extend it. Restore it. And inspire it.

Extending trust, that is, the propensity to trust, rekindles our spirits, both theirs and ours. It brings happiness to relationships, results to work, and confidence to our personal and professional lives.

Indeed, we should live by *the speed of trust.*

All is well. We are complete. And so it is.

To a propensity to trust,
Dr. Crystal

## Notes

[1] S. M. R. Covey, The speed of trust: The one thing that changes everything, (New York, NY: Free Press, 2006), 317.
[2] Covey, Speed of Trust, 316.
[3] Covey, Speed of Trust, 318.
[4] Covey, Speed of Trust, 318.
[5] Covey, Speed of Trust, 320.

kkk

*Crystal J. Davis*

# A FORCE FOR GOOD: THE DALAI LAMA'S VISION FOR OUR WORLD
by Daniel Goleman

Crystal J. Davis

# 20

# A FORCE FOR GOOD

*"Compassion is not religious business, it is human business, it is not a luxury, it is essential for our own peace and mental stability, it is essential for human survival."*

~Dalai Lama XIV[1]

Welcome back and thank you for returning to our 'Leading.From.Within' learning blog! I am happy and extremely grateful for each of you that have read and supported the blog. This week we begin our new 12-week series based on the book, *A Force for Good: The Dalai Lama's Vision for Our World* by Daniel Goleman.[2] Goleman is a wonderful writer and captures the heart of the Dalai Lama's vision of compassion for the world. Goleman has written more than a dozen books focused on emotional intelligence. He has moderated three meetings between the Dalai Lama and scientists, psychotherapists, and social activists to gain further insight into emotional intelligence and compassion. If you want to participate more actively (above the level of reading the weekly blog), please visit www.joinaforce4good.org and share your story. Now, let us begin…

Servant-leaders understand that compassion is one of the core competencies of authentic leadership. With a positive inner shift in consciousness, we can more naturally embody a real concern for others—that is, act with **compassion**. In doing so, servant-leaders are prepared to envision and act upon a larger mission with new zeal, clarity, calm, and a caring consciousness.

I would like to provide us with an overview of the Force for Good *vision* this week, and then we will delve into the 12 chapters of the book, gleaning insight and power therein on the concept of compassion.

There are eight key points in the **Force for Good** vision, all of which lead to compassionate action. These are taken straight from the Force for Good website. In the next 12 weeks, we will get into these concepts more deeply. It might be helpful to print this so that as we go through the book, you can jot down important thoughts, points, or ideas that resonate within you.

## Understanding the Force

### Free the mind and the heart

- Being calm, clear, and kind can enable us to act more effectively for a better world.
- Understand our emotional patterns-our personal map.
- Practice 'emotional hygiene' to minimize the spread of destructive feelings.
- Pause before acting on impulse.
- Combine a calm mind with a warm, giving heart.

### Embody compassion

- We have an innate capacity for compassion that we can strengthen to reach the widest circle.
- Humans have an innate need both to give, and to receive affection.
- Caring for others improves our own emotional state.
- Our 'circle of concern' can gradually extend beyond our own group to include all people.
- Compassion is a crucial moral rudder as we tackle the world's problems.

### Educate the heart

- Teach practical tools for handling destructive emotions and for living by a compassionate ethic.
- Education should be rooted in both knowledge and ethics.
- Social and emotional learning should be based on sound science.
- Techniques for emotional self-mastery are as fundamental as math.
- An ethics-based education is one key to solving our global problems.

**Oppose injustice**

- Compassion can be tough-minded, rooting out corruption with transparency and accountability.
- Do not allow anger to be a spur to action; compassion, not anger, is a better guide.
- Act without hatred or resorting to violence.
- When confronting injustice, oppose the act but do not give up on the person.
- Recognize that restraint and nonviolence are not signs of weakness, but of strength.

**Choose humane economics**

- Compassionate economics benefits everyone, and businesses can do good while doing well.
- Loving relationships of all kinds, and meaningful work which yields more than money, are keys to happiness.
- Economic freedom can be balanced with selfless service.
- Humane economic policy is guided by compassion, not self-interest.
- Businesses cannot be a force for good when profit is the only yardstick for success.

**Help those in need**

- Help those in need, whether with direct aid or by helping them help themselves.

- Recognize that the origins of poverty are not just circumstance but also a mind-set.
- Give people the tools they need to help themselves.
- Advocate against the inequitable social policies that cause poverty and dislocation.
- Support the advancement of women in leadership roles.

## Heal the earth

- Knowing the hidden links between human habits and ecology can reveal powerful ways to heal the earth.
- Advocate for 'radical transparency' that exposes the ecological impacts of what we buy and do.
- Embrace tools that measure the ecological 'true cost' of a product or service.
- Encourage finding better solutions to manmade problems and remain focused on progress—not doom and gloom.
- Extend our compassion to include both people and the planet, in equal measure.

## Connect across divides

- A peaceful world starts inside and uses dialogue to resolve conflicts.
- War cannot resolve differences; only dialogue can.
- The traits that unite humans far outnumber the differences that divide them.
- Hatred is learned and can be unlearned.
- True compassion has no national, ethnic, religious, or sectarian boundaries.

Servant-leaders intuitively recognize that beginning this social evolution, *living as compassion,* inside our own hearts and minds first is the life-long journey of a servant leader. It is the enlightened way to begin living as compassion. And in the end, the Dalai Lama says it's all about interdependence.

Martin Luther King, Jr. saw it through the lens of interdependence as well. He puts it this way, "We are caught in an inescapable network of mutuality, tied in a single garment of destiny. Whatever affects one directly, affects all indirectly."[3]

And so, we begin our journey into compassion. What it is. How we get there personally and globally. And the payoff is for us all.

To the force for good,
Dr. Crystal

## Notes

1  http://www.dalailamaquotes.org/
2  Daniel Goleman, *A force for good: The Dalai Lama's vision for our world*, (New York, NY: Bantam Books, 2009).
3  Goleman, *A force for good*, 5.

# 21

# REINVENT THE FUTURE

*"Whether you believe in God or not does not matter so much, whether you believe in Buddha or not does not matter so much; as a Buddhist, whether you believe in reincarnation or not does not matter so much. You must lead a good life. And a good life does not mean just good food, good clothes, good shelter. These are not sufficient. A good motivation is what is needed: compassion, without dogmatism, without complicated philosophy; just understanding that others are human brothers and sisters and respecting their rights and human dignity."*

~Dalai Lama XIV[1]

Servant-leaders understand that vision is what helps to move us forward in leadership as well as in our lives. Jonathan Swift characterizes vision saying it, "is the art of seeing things invisible to other people."[2] So does the Dalai Lama in the book, *A force for Good: The Dalai Lama's Vision for Our World* by Daniel Goleman. In the chapter, *Reinvent the Future*, Goleman provides The Dalai Lama's vision for a force for good.[3] Our journey provides us with the key points that represent a set of interlocking scenarios that articulate the Dalai Lama's vision with living examples, people, and projects that are already making his vision a reality.

## Emotional hygiene

Emotional hygiene is about taking responsibility for better managing our minds and emotions. It is about lessening the power of destructive emotions and fostering more positive modes of being. This kind of self-mastery allows us to target better, cultivate, and act on human values that form a universal ethic whereby the oneness of humanity is expressed as compassion toward all. This universal ethic does not look toward any religion or ideology, but rather grounds this worldview in empirical findings. The Dalai Lama calls it a science of compassion.

## Muscular compassion

Muscular compassion acts to expose and hold accountable toxic social forces such as corruption, collusion, and bias. Compassion in this area helps us to upgrade systems such as economics, politics, and science. In action, this compassion can bring in transparency, fairness, and accountability in everything that we do in the stock market, financing an election, or in reporting data.

## Compassionate economy

A compassionate economy reflects concern for all. In the realm of economics, compassion leads to focusing on how goods are distributed, not just on how to accumulate them. So that from compassion, there is created an imperative to care for those in need – the poor, the powerless, and the disenfranchised. But this means going beyond charity to empower those in need to begin to take care of themselves with dignity.

## Heal the planet

Human activity of all kinds is degrading the global systems that support life on this planet. We must begin to heal the planet.

## Education of the heart

We should help students cultivate tools for self-mastery and caring so that they can live with these human values. If such an education becomes universal and standard, the future generations would naturally act with compassion.

## Take a long view of history

We are urged to take a long view of history but to **act now** towards fulfilling this vision in any way we can, using whatever means we have at hand. Of course, these changes will take generations but even if we do not live to see the fulfillment, we can start this evolution toward compassion.

Taken together, these interlocking scenarios are synergistic, the whole being greater that any single part. Indeed, we can change the course through compassion for navigating our lives and our society for a better tomorrow.

What is presented offers us an opportunity to live our lives with generosity, discernment, and joy, rather than false fulfillment through money, power, and fame. In the coming weeks, we will encounter people and projects that are already signaling how we might move from vision to action. The Dalai Lama inspired some; others simply align with his vision.

In articulating his vision to us, the Dalai Lama speaks to us not from his religious role but by wearing the hat of a global leader, a futurist of sorts, who genuinely cares about the well-being of every person on the planet.

Servant-leaders know that the more altruistic the guiding values, the longer the time horizon, and the broader the human needs a leader addresses, the greater that leader's vision can be. Transformative leaders who are servant-leaders possess a transcendent purpose, pointing the way to a new reality. This is what the Dalai Lama's vision is all about.

Everyone one of us can be a force for good.

To reinventing the future,
Dr. Crystal

## Notes

[1] http://www.dalailamaquotes.org/

2 J. Swift, *A Modest Proposal and Other Satirical Works,* (Mineola, NY: Dover Publications, Inc., 1996).

[3] Daniel Goleman, *A force for good: The Dalai Lama's vision for our world,* (New York, NY: Bantam Books, 2009).

## 22

## EMOTIONAL HYGIENE

*"Now there are many, many people in the world, but relatively few with whom we interact, and even fewer who cause us problems. So, when you come across such a chance for practicing patience and tolerance, you should treat it with gratitude. It is rare. Just as having unexpectedly found a treasure in your own house, you should be happy and grateful toward your enemy for providing you that precious opportunity. Because if you are ever to be successful in your practice of patience and tolerance, which are critical factors in counteracting negative emotions, it is due to your own efforts and also the opportunity provided by your enemy."*

~Dalai Lama XIV[1]

Servant-leaders understand that emotional intelligence is a key competency of servant leadership. So, does the Dalai Lama in Chapter Two of the book, *A Force for Good: The Dalai Lama's Vision for Our World* by Daniel Goleman. The Dalai Lama calls this **emotional hygiene** and says that we should caution against, 'the enemies of our well-being' that are negative feelings.[2] These either lead us to harm ourselves or others, or undermine us through inner turbulence, and by hijacking our mental freedom.

One enemy of our well-being can be our attitude. It is necessary to check our internal thermometer to gauge how we are feeling. Our mental freedom is important to our sense of peace because as the Dalai Lama puts it, "an unruly, agitated human mind, given the fits of rage, malice, obsessive craving, jealousy, or arrogance can ruin lives."[3] By minding our feelings, we can face them head-on. That is a first step to managing them.

### Minding our feelings
Becoming aware of our feelings helps to offset what the Dalai Lama calls an **emotional hijack**. One method to handle rocky emotions is to notice

the emotional stirrings that signal destructive emotions, and then to analyze what those emotions mean (mindfulness). Using a fresh or a different perspective of our feelings rather than the same old thoughts that usually go with the emotions, can help us control an emotional hijack.

When we handle turbulent emotions, it helps us understand the build-up to them. If we can understand the build-up to the emotional hijack (what happens leading to it), then we can short-circuit what otherwise would become a huge emotional hijack. How do we get there?

## Getting there

Psychologists Phillip Shaver and Mario Mikulincer met with the Dalai Lama and talked about their experiments on how to evoke security-based feelings, that is more kindness, even in people whose feelings are stuck in insecure patterns.[4] What they found is people who are insecure tend to be less tolerant of other groups and are less likely to act altruistically and are less compassionate.

The psychologists concluded that helping people shift into a more secure sense of self, into a more positive state, made insecure people show a greater willingness to help someone. They became more compassionate.

Words such as 'love' triggered a kind of attachment that made people more mentally available; staying bound to their insecurity only made them susceptible to a sea of negative feelings. A secure state of consciousness (being) diminished destructive emotions (emotional hijack) and amplified positive ones.

The Dalai Lama argues that cultivating a greater control over our inner world is a potential for everyone and in this way, we can lessen our destructive feelings such as anger, fear, and suspicion. It is all about becoming mindful of negative thoughts. Understanding where we are and where we want to go in our internal world, is critical to servant-leaders. We could use a map to help us.

## A map of the emotions

The Dalai Lama envisions that one day we will have a map similar to an airline map for air travel; it would guide us through managing our emotions with compassion.

It is important to know which emotions are helpful and which can become destructive, how they both develop, and the connections between them. The more we know about emotions, the better we can handle them. This is why a map of emotions can be helpful.

It is also important to note that no emotion is either good or bad. They are all useful in life. Fears can be valid in that they mobilize us to face an actual threat. On the other hand, it can be destructive if it is a paralyzing distortion of reality or a wildly exaggerated misperception, as seen in agoraphobia.

Servant-leaders understand that the spectrum of emotions that run from our well-being to those that destroy, offer the main coordinates for our inner terrain. It is helpful to understand both the up and the downs because sometimes when we are so fixated on what is upsetting us, we have no bandwidth left to notice others or to empathize with them.

We are invited to become more aware (mindful) of where our moods are coming from. We must delve deeper into the real causes and conditions of our destructive emotions. The Dalai Lama says whether we are guided by such a map or any other useful method, each of us is capable of making small improvement. A recent book on meditation says that even if it just makes us, "ten percent happier," we can begin by dealing with our own inner confusion and find a path to greater happiness.[5]

## Cultivating Emotional Balance (CEB)

The CEB program integrates equal parts of Tibetan contemplative traditions and modern psychology to help people balance emotions. Eve Ekman, a medical social worker shared her study of a CEB program with 60 inmates at the Soledad State Prison in Monterrey Bay, California.[6] What she found was that when the prisoners were able to map their emotions (most had never felt loved, cared for, or connected, had found solace in drugs, and had led a life filled with fear, anger, and hurt), they were able to step back from their emotional turmoil to see what they needed to release destructive feelings.

Guided contemplation offered the inmates tools for managing their inner worlds better. Five questions guided the meditation:

1. What would it be like for me to attain genuine happiness?
2. What would I need from the world to achieve this?
3. What would I need from myself to achieve this?
4. What habits would I need to learn?
5. How could I bring this to the world and be of service?[7]

Another practice Ekman used with the inmates was to focus on the sensation of their breathing. She called it resting on their inner refuge without worrying about the past or about the future. She asked them not to dwell on the difficult, regretful past, but to use the present moment to set a new motivation, a new aspiration. For many of the inmates, this practice was liberating. The session closed with inmates silently wishing each person well in their lives.

When Goleman last spoke to Ekman, she was going back to the prison to train three of the inmates from that day to teach the CEB program to anyone else who might be interested.

As can be seen, the CEB draws on some points that the Dalai Lama emphasizes; it controls our emotional impulses, imparts a scientific understanding of emotions as well as provides for contemplative tools that provide a way to cultivate a sense of ease.

Servant-leaders understand that becoming cool and clear certainly does help our well-being, but that alone will not help us in the service of a force for good.

For that, something more is needed – a moral compass.

To emotional well-being,
Dr. Crystal

## Notes

1  http://www.dalailamaquotes.org/
2  Daniel Goleman, *A force for good: The Dalai Lama's vision for our world*, (New York, NY: Bantam Books, 2009), 28.
3  Goleman, *Force for good*, 30.
4  Goleman, *Force for good*, 35.
5  Goleman, *Force for good*, 40.
6  Goleman, *Force for good*, 41.
7  Goleman, *Force for good*, 42.

## 23

## THE KINDNESS REVOLUTION

*"My religion is kindness."*

~Dalai Lama XIV[1]

Servant-leaders understand that kindness is the way for an authentic leader. In Goleman's book, *A Force for Good: The Dalai Lama's Vision for Our World*, Chapter Three, *The Kindness Revolution*, the Dalai Lama tells a story, in a room filled with eight thousand people at Emory University in Atlanta.[2] The story is that of a gentleman by the name of Richard Moore who was blinded by a rubber bullet fired by a British soldier during the trouble in Northern Ireland.

Remarkably, Moore got over his self-pity and forgave the soldier. Moore was in the audience that night and much to the dismay of the State Department security, the Dalai Lama walked off the stage into the crowd and greeted Moore in the Tibetan gesture of mutual respect. "*Love, love, love,*" said the Dalai Lama, "I call him my hero! You know, your sight can be taken away, but not your vision."[3]

Richard Moore went on to finish his university education and he founded the *Children in Crossfire*, an organization that seeks to better the lives of children in countries such as Tanzania, Ethiopia, and Gambia—those children who have been caught up in the war. What is amazing about this is that the Dalai Lama's (a person that millions of people idealize) message is compassion and forgiveness, and he sees Moore as a personal hero. Fascinating!

In another story of compassion, Goleman narrated the incident of when the Dalai Lama was told that he had won the Nobel Peace Prize. When asked by the reporters, "How does it feel to win the Nobel Prize?" the Dalai Lama responded, "I am happy...for those who wanted me to win the prize." And when he learned about the money that came with the prize, the Dalai Lama immediately thought of whom he would give it to.

The Dalai Lama is not asking us to be kinder because he says so. He is calling us to a deeper awareness and consciousness, arguing that our emotional world affects the people around us and leads to a more compassionate outlook. The moment you think of others, your mind widens, says the Dalai Lama.

Here's a summary of the chapter.

## Beyond religion

A European preacher once told the Dalai Lama that compassion can only come through faith and through God's blessing. The Dalai Lama argued that he had heard that animals such as dolphins and elephants could show compassion. Even dogs and cats could be compassionate, and that was not through faith.

The Dalai Lama challenges the assumptions that he is solely a religious figure. He understands human suffering from his deep spiritual reflections, but as a world leader, he envisions the larger world perspective.

Finding compassion as a common theme in the world's religion, the Dalai Lama seeks to engage a common agreement amongst all of us – amongst those of us who have faith and those who do not – about a set of human ethical values that promote qualities such as compassion, forgiveness, self-discipline, and contentment.

## The case for compassion

Compassion has been studied scientifically, and research by the *National Institute of Mental Health* indicated that children before the age of two show compassion. Children are universally attuned to another child's distress and most often will try to comfort them. The Dalai Lama says that children, "already know the map of emotions" especially when their parents are compassionate.[4]

Parents direct a toddler's attention to empathy when they say, "Look how sad you made her feel" rather than, "You were naughty when you hit her." The Dalai Lama believes, and science proves, that innate ethical compassion is a biological feature of our species.

## Wise selfish

Wise selfish means that we see our own well-being in that of everyone else's. The Dalai Lama says that self-focus has become so excessive that we become oblivious to other's needs. Self-focus

1. narrows our vision,
2. limits broad thinking and consciousness, and
3. affects our immune system, leaving us open to a variety of diseases.

Indeed, compassion reduces fear, boosts confidence, and opens us to our inner strength.

Goleman told of a story where he and his wife had some unexpected downtime with the Dalai Lama. When his wife asked what he had been doing, the Dalai Lama replied, "shopping." Taken aback, as the Dalai Lama **never** shops, she asked, "What for?" The Dalai Lana replied, "a toy for my cat."[5]

Someone had given the Dalai Lama a tiny, wobbly stray kitten and the Dalai Lama knew it would have died if he left it on the street, so he had taken it in. His heart warmed at the thought of the love the little kitten had for him.

## A sense of oneness

The Dalai Lama treats everyone with respect. Goleman told of how the Dalai Lama was waiting backstage for the mayor of San Francisco as he was delayed offering an official welcome to the city. Although there were a handful of dignitaries waiting nearby, the Dalai Lama made a beeline to one of the stagehands to chat it up. On another occasion, when the Dalai Lama was visiting Mikhail Gorbachev, he paused and went over to shake hands with the guard at the door.

The guard later said that in the 25 years he had been standing there, no dignitary had so much as noticed him; yet the Dalai Lama had shaken his hand. The Dalai Lama treats everyone with respect, "whether high officials or beggars-no difference, no distinctions."[6]

The Dalai Lama challenges us to model a person-to-person caring with the understanding that we are all the same beneath ethnicity, nationality, religion, gender, and the like.

The Dalai Lama says, "If I were to say, I'm his Holiness, the Dalai Lama" imitating a pompous, puffed-up person, "then I am in a prison. The sense of being special is a form of self-deception. Whenever I talk to a few people or thousands, I consider them and myself the same—same emotions, same body. Then we feel a closeness."[7]

Understanding our shared humanity leads to compassion for everyone.

## Loving everyone

People all over the world admire the Dalai Lama for how he embodies qualities such as humility, resilience, and compassion. But, Goleman wondered as to who inspired the Dalai Lama? The first person he names is Shantideva, an eighth-century Indian sage whose book, *A Guide to the Bodhisattva's Way of Life* is a complete program of ethical discipline and mental training, designed to achieve unstinting compassion.

The Dalai Lama advises that anyone can practice compassion—even for our enemies-but it is no easy feat. Each day, we should try to be compassionate, to have the right motivations and to approach it with common sense and good reasoning (no religion required). But, for those who hold and practice religious faith, reason can deepen existing convictions. And now **science** provides us with a universal path to embrace compassion.

To the kindness revolution,
Dr. Crystal

## Notes

[1] http://www.dalailamaquotes.org/

2  Daniel Goleman, *A force for good: The Dalai Lama's vision for our world*, (New York, NY: Bantam Books, 2009), 44.
3  Goleman, *Force for good*, 44.
4  Goleman, *Force for good*, 51.
5  Goleman, *Force for good*, 52.
6  Goleman, *Force for good*, 56.
7  Goleman, *Force for good*, 57.

Crystal J. Davis

24

PARTNERING WITH SCIENCE

*"As my comprehension of science has grown, it has gradually become evident to me that, insofar as understanding the physical world is concerned, there are many areas of traditional Buddhist thought where our explanations and theories are rudimentary when compared with those of modern science. But, at the same time, even in the most highly developed scientific countries, it is clear that human beings continue to experience suffering, especially at the emotional and psychological level."*

The Universe in a Single Atom by Dalai Lama XIV[1]

Servant-leaders understand that science has a place concerning compassion. The Dalai Lama argues in the book, *A Force for Good: The Dalai Lama's Vision for Our World*, Chapter Four, *Partnering with Science*, that compassion, seen through the lens of spirituality and science, can speak to a broader number of people than any religious faith can. "If I offer methods from Buddhism," says the Dalai Lama, "people will dismiss it as just religion." But if science says their methods work, "then people have more openness."

Over the years, the Dalai Lama has made acquaintances and even close friends with many scientists and psychologists and their work in compassion; Dr. Richard Davidson, (who founded the *Center for Investigating Healthy Minds*), British quantum physicist David Bohm, German physicist Carl Friedrich von Weizsäcker, philosopher Karl Popper, Paul Ekman, and a host of others.

What the Dalai Lama appreciates is that science is not based on differences in faith or nationality. He finds a genuine sense of internationalism among the great scientists of the world. If science helps us with findings and research that help us create greater well-being and lessen destructive emotions, then it helps us and the scientists.

A more provocative argument that the Dalai Lama makes is, that today's psychological science is at a mere '*kindergarten*' level when it comes to mapping the mind. He says that modern psychology needs to develop more knowledge and methods for dealing with destructive emotions.

He speaks about the ancient 'Indian psychology' that is found in the text of the *Abhidharma*, that explains the dynamics of the consciousness mind.[3] A key dynamic of this text is that when one possesses a healthy, wholesome mind, the destructive emotions disappear.

The Dalai Lama believes that if we can weld ancient wisdom with contemporary scientific findings, then we can create a larger map of the mind. He has even been instrumental in bringing science to the traditional Tibetan monastic education. Working with Emory University, science textbooks are being translated for inclusion in the Tibetan educational curriculum.

More than that, The Dalai Lama has always said that followers should not accept his teachings out of blind faith or devotion, but rather through their own investigation and experiment, which is always more powerful than mere imagination or belief.

Similar to this perspective, is the Biblical verse in 2 Timothy 2:15 King James Version (KJV) which puts it this way, "Study to show thyself approved unto God, a workman that needeth not to be ashamed, rightly dividing the word of truth." He says in this way these methods are indeed scientific.

Another program supporting compassion research that has gained support and success, is the Compassion Cultivation Training or CCT from the Stanford University's School of Medicine. An evaluation of the 8-week program by University researchers found that for people who participated in the program, their worries were lessened while their happiness was increased. Those suffering from acute social phobia had less anxiety and fears; those who suffered from enduring chronic pain, their sensitivity to pain decreased after nine weeks and the sense of well-being improved— their spouses reported them being less angry.

The scientific findings that the Dalai Lama has found with compassion, drives him to use the evidence in his message of compassion. "If I say be compassionate," says the Dalai Lama, "then people will say, 'Of course, he says that—he's the Dalai Lama, he's Buddhist.' But if I can show scientific evidence of the benefits, then it's more convincing. People will pay attention."[4]

So, we see that compassion is not just a religious thing, but a scientific thing as well. But, putting compassion into action? Well, that is another thing.

To the science of compassion,
Dr. Crystal

## Notes

[1]  http://www.dalailamaquotes.org/
[2]  Daniel Goleman, *A force for good: The Dalai Lama's vision for our world*, (New York, NY: Bantam Books, 2009), 66.
[3]  Goleman, *Force for good*, 67.
[4]  Goleman, *Force for good*, 79.

# 25

# A MUSCULAR COMPASSION

*"Compassion naturally creates a positive atmosphere, and as a result you feel peaceful and content."*

~Dalai Lama XIV[1]

Servant-leaders understand that the type of compassion the Dalai Lama is teaching, is more than a soft and flabby kind of compassion. The Dalai Lama argues in the book, *A Force for Good: The Dalai Lama's Vision for Our World*, Chapter Five, A Muscular Compassion, that three principles that exemplify compassion in action are *fairness* (treating everyone the same), which depends on *transparency* (being honest and open), and *accountability* (being answerable for misdeeds).[2]

Compassion that takes action, becomes and is active in helping the poor and marginalized people. The Dalai Lama notes the exemplary action of Pope Francis's call for church officials to live more simply.

So much so, that he wrote a letter of admiration to the Pope, when he demoted the German Bishop, Franz-Peter Tebartz-van Elst, who spent more than $43 million dollars on his private residence, including bronze window frames, a $30,000 bathtub, and a one-million-dollar landscaping job.[3] In the second letter to the Pope, the Dalai Lama expressed his appreciation for his "tough stand, which carried a real teaching of Jesus Christ."[4]

Constructive anger can be beneficial to compassion and action. Summoning the positive aspects of anger, such as a strong focus, extra energy, and determination, can make our response to injustice more effective. The Dalai Lama recalls a story in which a social worker told him that she and a group of her colleagues were angry at the huge caseloads they were given; this overwhelmed their ability to be effective and successful with their clients.

The initial anger they felt for the lack of quality care for the children they were supposed to be helping, mobilized them. So, the social workers rallied in protest and got their caseloads lowered. Indeed, as the Dalai Lama points out, "a modicum of anger helps us stand up against unfairness. Moral outrage can drive positive action."

The Dalai Lama speaks of equanimity and says that if it eludes us, then we are unable to protect ourselves against a real threat. "Keep a calm mind, study the situation, then take a countermeasure. If you let a wrongdoing happen, it might continue and increase, so, out of compassion, take appropriate countermeasures."[5]

Last night, I watched the 2008 movie, *Gran Torino* starring Clint Eastwood. As I think about the muscular compassion that the Dalia Lama speaks about in this chapter, I couldn't help thinking about the ending of the movie where Walt Kowalski (played by Cling Eastwood) chooses to give his life to save the Hmong family against the constant threat of the gangs in the neighborhood.

An ultimate sacrifice and show of Muscular Compassion, Kowalski could have easily dispelled of the gang in another way, yet he takes an ultimate attitude of compassion, sacrificing his own life.

In the last part of the chapter, the Dalai Lama speaks of impeccability. He tells of when he changed the name of his group that handles the funds he donates from The Dalai Lama Trust to the Dalai Lama *Charitable* Trust. In India as in Britain, the word 'trust' means charitable organizations. The Dalai Lama did not realize that in America, 'a trust' could mean a fund set up to avoid taxes on money that benefits oneself.

Understanding this, he immediately suggested changing the name so that it would be clear that the trust was set up to benefit others as philanthropy rather than self-interest. The Dalai Lama seeks transparency, fairness, and accountability in all that he does, and he wishes the same for each of us.

In the end, one realization for human happiness is interdependence. This is what the Dalai Lama wrote in the foreword to a biography of

Mahatma Gandhi. "Our own successful or happy future is very much related to that of others."[6]

As we begin to lessen destructive emotions, we can use long-term strategies that enhance Muscular Compassion. What we want are systems that have transparency, fairness, and accountability. In this way, compassion is action!

To muscular compassion,
Dr. Crystal

## Notes

[1] http://www.dalailamaquotes.org/

[2] Daniel Goleman, *A force for good: The Dalai Lama's vision for our world*, (New York, NY: Bantam Books, 2009), 84.

[3] Goleman, *Force for good*, 85.

[4] Goleman, *Force for good*, 85.

[5] Goleman, *Force for good*, 98.

*Crystal J. Davis*

## 26

## ECONOMICS AS IF PEOPLE MATTERED

*"We need to employ a secular approach to ethics, secular in the Indian sense of respecting all religious traditions and even the views of non-believers in an unbiased way. Secular ethics rooted in scientific findings, common experience, and common sense can easily be introduced into the secular education system. If we can do that, there is a real prospect of making this 21st century an era of peace and compassion".*

~Dalai Lama XIV[1]

Servant-leaders understand the need for ethical values in their work. In the capitalist world, the acquisition of wealth is at the exclusion of concern for the other's well-being and capitalism lacks a compassionate moral outlook. This is what the Dalai Lama argues in the book, *A Force for Good: The Dalai Lama's Vision for Our World*, Chapter Six, Economics as if People Mattered.[2]

Capitalism, as the Dalai Lama sees it, assumes that people are only interested in self and profit, profit, profit. The financial systems are focused largely on rewards and greed while ignoring the consequences to people and the planet. What is worse is that all of this is happening while extreme poverty is glaring us in the face.

The Dalai Lama believes that it is not capitalism or socialism that is the problem, but rather a moral principle of the people involved in these systems.

An economics that works for everyone is one that is, a compassionate economy, and mixes an entrepreneurial spirit with a sound social support system, as well as taxes on wealth, similar to that of Sweden's economy.

In Thomas Piketty's book, *Capital*, he argues that those with money which they can invest, will always earn more than those who work for their wages. In this way, capitalism helps the rich stay rich, far more than it helps ordinary workers.

91

Indeed, a healthy economy is not determined by how many billionaires there are, but by the well-being of everyone.

Capitalism can be a force for good if it has a genuine concern for all.

Goleman tells of a story when the Dalai Lama was informed about the growing number of billionaires. When he asked, through his translator, Thupten Jinpa, "Why would anyone want that much money?" After all, he said, "You only have one stomach."[3]

## Rethinking economics

What would an economics driven by our neural system—caring and contentment—and not a brain system that drives people's decision about their money (the threat that worries about safety), look like? Well, some economists are already exploring this possibility. Early researchers in this area, Adam Smith, and Jeremy Bentham, studied economic theory from the perspective of success for an economy concerned about the well-being of its people.

Lord Richard Layard, London School of Economics, became interested in this type of economics too. Layard contends that the ballooning wealth of a small few masks the low well-being of the masses.

## Nations that rank high on creating wealth rank low on measures of well-being.

For example, if two parents spend long hours at work to pay for day-care for their children, the profit that the day-care makes adds to the overall GDP (gross domestic product), but the stress on the parents and family are largely ignored. Their sense of well-being...lost.

## The secret to happiness

The Dalai Lama tells of a story of when he visited Princeton University for a lecture, and a student asked him, "What is the source of happiness?" He looked around at the students waiting for an answer and he replied, "Money! Sex! Nightclubs!" His joke brought the house down.[4]

The Dalai Lama did get serious and told the students that they might feel a temporary relief in material things and experiences, but when something causes us to worry or fear we tend to forget the happiness. This is why he argues, we need a deeper basis for contentment. He tells the students that feeling kindness, affection, and trust within our circle of family and friends, makes us happier than luxuries.

### Action for happiness
Gus O'Donnell, a former Cabinet Secretary of UK, and Lord Richard Layard, created the secular movement and website, *Action for Happiness* (http://www.actionforhappiness.org/). In *Exploring What Matters,* an eight-week course of the Action for Happiness organization, the group focuses on one single question. People from all over the world connect and initiate small local groups, and each meeting ends with people choosing an action to promote happiness and well-being. One group started the Happiness Café where like-minded people came together and shared ideas on how to create greater happiness. Action for Happiness is based on ten keys for happier living. Visit their website to take the happiness pledge.

### Doing good while doing well
The Dalai Lama was delighted to hear about Greyston Bakery, a for-benefit corporation in Yonkers, New York, who hires, trains, and houses homeless people, ex-convicts, drug addicts, battered wives, illiterates, and helps them gain an honest livelihood.

The bakery supplies its brownies to Ben & Jerry's ice-cream factory in Vermont. Greyston Bakery is a B Corporation (businesses that have an explicit mission to benefit society or the environment, as well as to make a profit) whose motto is, "We don't hire people to bake brownies; we bake brownies to hire people." There are many more B Corporations in the United States that re-create capitalism to be meaningful and not just profitable. They are essentially businesses that become **a force for good**.

"The global economy," Says the Dalai Lama, "is like a roof over all of us. But it depends on individual pillars for support." Like he ended his speech with the college students at Princeton, "First take care of yourself financially. Then, step by step, stand on your own feet in order to help others."[5]

To positive economics,
Dr. Crystal

## Notes

[1]  http://www.dalailamaquotes.org/
[2]  Daniel Goleman, *A force for good: The Dalai Lama's vision for our world*, (New York, NY: Bantam Books, 2009), 87.
[3]  Goleman, *Force for good*, 101.
[4]  Goleman, *Force for good*, 106.
[5]  Goleman, *Force for good*, 117.

# 27

# CARE FOR THOSE IN NEED

*"If we develop concern for other people's welfare, share other people's suffering, and help them, ultimately we will benefit. If we think only of ourselves, and forget about others, ultimately, we will lose. The more we care for the happiness of others, the greater our own sense of well-being becomes."*

~ Dalai Lama XIV[1]

Servant-leaders understand the value of care and concern for others. Translating compassion into action requires pure motivation and an understanding of the root causes of the dynamics that creates the problem. This is what the Dalai Lama argues in the book, *A Force for Good: The Dalai Lama's Vision for Our World*, Chapter Seven, **Care for Those in Need**.[2]

The Dalai Lama makes an excellent case for compassion. He says if you believe in God, then you know that all seven billion people in the world are equal and have the same nature and the same right to happiness. Servant-leaders who care for others, particularly the weak, are serving God.

For persons with no religious belief, the Dalai Lama presents another approach. He says that we are social animals, and even animals sometimes practice generosity. They share their food and care for each other. So, if you have plenty to share, and you are happy, but your neighbor has challenges, it is entirely natural to share and to be generous. In whatever way you think, we must help and serve people; we must develop and live generosity,' says Dalai Lama.[3]

The Dalia Lama outlines the rest of Chapter Seven under three core themes: Help people help themselves, achieve self-mastery, and make women the leaders. A summary describes the rest of Chapter Seven.

## Help people help themselves

The Dalia Lama tells the story of Baba Amte, a former Gandhi follower and his competent care and concern for the *Anandwan community* in Western India. *Anandwan* is a village of homes, schools, workshops, and a hospital this was built on desolate land, created entirely by people with leprosy and other disabilities.

Today, Baba cares for over 2,000 leprosy victims, blind and deaf-mute people, and orphans born to unwed mothers.

Baba Amte's vision is that "charity destroys, work builds."[4] He spoke to the Dalai Lama about the people's self-confidence and positive mental attitude. He said that "their work gives them confidence and self-respect, so they are full of enthusiasm."[5]

The Dalai Lama emphasized that the root causes of people's difficulties have to change. People have been told, especially the poor, that they can't do much for themselves. And when they began to believe in this propaganda, it becomes true to them.

The Dalai Lama spoke of when Chinese Communist officials spread a propaganda saying that Tibetan brains were 'inferior.' Many Tibetans adopted this self-defeating view. But when they were given the same schooling and chances in life, Tibetans did as well as anybody else.

## Self-mastery

Servant-leaders realize the value of education, training and equipment when seeking to help impoverished areas such as India and Africa. The Dalai Lama speaks of Mellody Hobson's story, the youngest of six children (her oldest sibling more than 20 years her senior) to an African-American single mother in Chicago.[6]

She spoke of the overwhelming sense of financial insecurity they had faced. She recalls the incident when they went grocery shopping and her mother's 'insufficient funds' check was taped to the checkout counter; this was done as a warning to cashiers to not accept a check from them.

Hobson remembers her mother preaching and instilling an indomitable spirit in her telling her that she could achieve anything with hard work. Her living example was her ambition and industriousness; she would buy run-down buildings at cheap rates and then fix them up.

Hobson internalized her mother's teachings. She would lock herself in the bathroom to complete her studies, and to drown out the household noise. Hobson was always at the top of her class. She attended The Ogden School, a school with high academic standards and an International Baccalaureate program.

Eventually, Hobson went on to Princeton University. There, she wrote her thesis on South African children suffering under apartheid. Their struggles deeply resonated with Hobson.

She landed her first job (a rarity among the 1,100 other graduates in her Princeton class) with Ariel Investments and worked her way up, and at 31 years old, became president.

She established a program called *After School Matters*, a program that serves 22, 000 inner city kids from Chicago. In the end, Hobson says it was about mindset, and this is what *After School Matters* teaches.

Economic research (a 30-year study on cognitive control), cited that the power to stay focused and ignore distractions, to delay gratification now in pursuit of a future goal, and to control destructive emotions, predicts children's future financial success and wealth better than does their IQ and the wealth of the family they grew up in.

The researchers call it cognitive control, mindset or grit. The Hindi concept of it is called *swaraj*: self-mastery or self-rule. Indeed, it is about perseverance in the face of adversity.

**Women as leaders**

Malala Yousafzai was shot in the head three times by Taliban extremists because she spoke out against the lack of education for girls. Her book, *I am Malala*, is a global bestseller and she became the youngest person to win a Nobel Prize for Peace.[7]

The Dalia Lama praised Malala and wrote to her saying, "That you have continued, unbowed, to promote the basic right to education earns only admiration."[8] The Dalai Lama urges female leadership for the future. He argues that our times require leaders who are sensitive to human needs and women are those leaders.

Servant-leaders know that care and concern for others are the cornerstones of this type of leadership. In this way, we all can be **a force for good**.

To care and concern,
Dr. Crystal

## Notes

[1] http://www.dalailamaquotes.org/

[2] Daniel Goleman, *A force for good: The Dalai Lama's vision for our world*, (New York, NY: Bantam Books, 2009), 118.

[3] Goleman, *Force for good*, 121.

[4] Goleman, *Force for good*, 122.

[5] Goleman, *Force for good*, 123.

[6] Goleman, *Force for good*, 125.

[7] Goleman, *Force for good*, 130.

[8] Goleman, *Force for good*, 131.

## 28

## HEAL THE EARTH

*"When seen from outer space, our beautiful blue planet has no national boundaries."*

~Dalai Lama[1]

Servant-leaders understand the value of care and concern for the earth. The environmental damage that the earth suffers today requires our immediate attention, not in some distant future with regard to cutting emissions and lowering the temperature of the earth. This is what the Dalai Lama argues in the book, *A Force for Good: The Dalai Lama's Vision for Our World*, Chapter Eight, Heal the Earth.[2]

The Dalai Lama is quoted as saying, "Many of the Earth's inhabitants, animals, plants, insects, and even micro-organisms that we know to be rare may not be known by future generations." We have the resources and the ability to act now. It is our responsibility, before it is too late. The ongoing ecological damage to the planet is creating another set, a different set, of powerless victims:

- species under risk of extinction,
- future generations who will live in very bad environmental conditions, and
- people of the poorest countries whose health and environment are disproportionately harmed by the consumption habits of America and the world.

The Dalai Lama has learned from top environmental researchers that our current geological age called *Anthropocene* (meaning 'human' in Greek) is the recognition of how humans and their activities have deteriorated the planet's life-support systems-two of the best known are the carbon cycle and global warming.

So, what should we do? How do we get ourselves out of this mess?

## Radical transparency

Because we as a human race are for the most part blind to our carbon footprints on Earth, the Dalai Lama says that we need a 'deeper transparency'-transparency with regard to, for example, the life cycle of the smart phone.

A cellular phone's life cycle today may begin with the mining of rare earths in China and Africa-some of those areas are controlled not by the government buy by militia that deploy slave labor. That same life cycle ends in a poor village somewhere in India, where the people are exposed to a toxic mix of cyanide because of the need to recover the valuable bits (gold) of the circuit boards.

An example of radical transparency is seen in the new software that makes it easier today to track the life cycle of cell phones and the companies that sell the ones that are the least harmful to the planet. This kind of transparency could alert us to how our purchases connect to the planet in a harmful or at least in the least harmful way.

## Educating our children

Education and transparency can help us to awaken to the knowledge and understanding of each of our individual responsibilities and accountabilities to heal the Earth. The Dalai Lama believes it is necessary to educate our children as he believes our children are open-minded and flexible and will understand the care of the planet as a natural part of life. We must take these steps before our eyes are stinging and our lungs are burning as then it may be far too late.

The Dalai Lama admits, "I am from the last century, and our generation created a lot of problems. The youth of this century are the planet's real humanity now. They can work together in the spirit of brotherhood and sisterhood to share ideas and find solutions. They are our real hope."[4]

Goleman tells the story of a teacher in Northhampton, Massachusetts who brought a small crate of clementines to share with her second-grade

100

class. The assignment was to think about all the people and places involved in getting those clementines to their classroom, and to send a silent good wish to them.

The students started thinking and when asked to call out the people, places and things involved in the clementine's arrival to their classroom, they began shouting out, the sun, the water, the people who grew the tree, the store people. They were getting it. They understood all of the people and things it took to get that clementine in their hands all the way from Morocco.

The teacher then asked them to peel it, feel it, and to put all of their focus on the clementine. This exercise in mindfulness allowed the students to pause and send good wishes to everyone who was involved in delivering the single clementine to their hands.

This exercise stretched those second-graders' minds in at least three ways:

- paying close attention to the clementine exercised the mental muscle of focus,
- wishing well to the people who made having the fruit possible and thanking them widened the circle of caring, and
- awareness of the chain of people who brought that fruit from Morocco to their school suggested systems thinking.[5]

In the end, servant-leaders understand and take the appropriate action to lessen their carbon footprint as individuals, educate our children as a community, and do what is necessary to heal the Earth.

To healing the earth,
Dr. Crystal

## Notes

1  http://www.dalailamaquotes.org/
2  Daniel Goleman, *A force for good: The Dalai Lama's vision for our world*, (New York, NY: Bantam Books, 2009), 137.
3  Goleman, *Force for good*, 140.
4  Goleman, *Force for good*, 152.
5  Goleman, *Force for good*, 152.

## 29

# THREE WAYS TO CREATE A WORLD THAT WORKS FOR EVERYONE

*"Given the scale of life in the cosmos, one human life is no more than a tiny blip. Each one of us is a just visitor to this planet, a guest, who will only stay for a limited time. What greater folly could there be than to spend this short time alone, unhappy or in conflict with our companions? Far better, surely, to use our short time here in living a meaningful life, enriched by our sense of connection with others and being of service to them."*

~ Dalai Lama XIV[1]

Servant-leaders understand the value of controlling the mind and emotions. Once we can feel compassion and move from unhappy and angry ways of acting, the *us-versus-them* mentality, then, we can live together peacefully. This is what the Dalai Lama argues in the book, *A Force for Good: The Dalai Lama's Vision for Our World*, Chapter Nine, **A Century of Dialogue**.[2]

The Dalai Lama is quoted as saying, "The initiative must come from the individual. In a change from a warrior-like society to a peaceful one at the worldwide level, the more peaceful world starts with the individual. Why? It takes an emotional change-compassion."[3]

The Dalai Lama believes that it takes three things to create a world that works for everyone:

- dialogue – does not mean we all agree but we will respect different views.
- negotiation – does mean forming partnerships of mutual respect and concern.
- patience – not a foolish patience but one that respects your needs and wishes.

The Dalai Lama told students at San Diego State University about the native chant that goes, "Your bone is my bone. Your blood is my blood." This attitude is one that reminds us of our profound interconnection and oneness of all of life. We should have an inclusive sensibility for the growing collective challenges we face in the 21st century.

So, what should we do? How do we create meaningful dialogue?

## The power of truth

The Dalai Lama argues that the world belongs to the people, not to kings, or queens, rulers, or government, and as such, they cannot remain forever. The people will always remain and herein lies the truth. The Dalai Lama speaks of Martin Luther King, Jr. and Mahatma Gandhi's message of nonviolence as clear examples of the power of truth, sincerity, and honesty.

And the Dalai Lama agrees that nonviolence may take longer to happen, but its long-term benefits are greater than violence. He uses the example of Gandhi and his greatest achievement of showing how nonviolence can be achieved and implemented effectively, not only in the political arena, but also in day-to-day living.

## Harmony among religions

The Dalai Lama speaks of harmony among religions by saying, "Those who possess the consciousness of us-and-them attitude on a basis of religion are distorting those beliefs."[5]What this attitude does is divide us from our essential nature of care and concern for one another with religion in service as hatred to one another. He says that instead of using our faith to build and our resources to transform the world and our personality and character, we impose that personality on religion. The Dalai Lama warns that it become very tricky when people manipulate religion. In the end, the real practice of faith is the practice of love-it is all the same.

## Toward a century of dialogue

One way to create a new dialogue is to reach out to those who are receptive, emphasizing the benefits in common for each side. By thinking, speaking, and living as, 'us', we can better enter into dialogue and negotiations that will leave everyone winners.

The Dalai Lama talks of such groups as the Forum 2000, a group of people from diverse countries, cultures, religions, and academic disciplines, who convene once a year to identify key global issues and look for ways to de-escalate conflicts. This is a positive step in the direction of compassion and dialogue. These key stakeholders are well-known and respected and come with no hidden agendas, willing and able to work as selfless servants for the greater good of society.

The Dalai Lama said that such groups represent a new kind of leadership in the world scene whereby there is no interest or ties to governments, but rather to the best interests of humanity. This body would represent billions of people in the world and its respect would lie in its respect of and the esteem people have for, its recommendations for world problems.

Such a group sounds like servant-leaders to me.

To a new dialogue,
Dr. Crystal

## Notes

[1]  http://www.dalailamaquotes.org/
[2]  Daniel Goleman, *A force for good: The Dalai Lama's vision for our world*, (New York, NY: Bantam Books, 2009), 153.
[3]  Goleman, *Force for good*, 155.
[4]  Goleman, *Force for good*, 157.
[5]  Goleman, *Force for good*, 167.

30

# FOUR WAYS TO EDUCATE THE HEART

*"When educating the minds of our youth, we should not forget to educate their hearts."*

~ Dalai Lama[1]

Servant-leaders understand that education today requires more than the standard textbook education or standard body of knowledge taught in the classroom. This education includes the basics of how the mind works, a healthy regulation of emotions, the cultivation of attention, mindfulness, empathy, and caring; learning to handle conflicts non-violently; and a sense of wholeness and oneness with all of life. What is needed today is an education of the heart with ethics and the capacity for living by compassion and values as essential. This is what the Dalai Lama argues in the book, *A Force for Good: The Dalai Lama's Vision for Our World*, Chapter Ten, **Educate the Heart**.[2]

### Mind training

The Dalai Lama coached a young student, an eleventh grader at Moberly High School who had on EEG headgear that was tracking her concentration. As she stayed focused, a line on the machine drifted upward. As her focus declined, the line drifted downward. Some of her friends were told to do things to distract her.

As the Dalai Lama began, the coach explained that when training the mind, one should make a distinction between the mental and sensory levels. When focusing in on an object, the work is both mental and eye consciousness. He said when you focus on what's in front of you, the mind can be limited as to what in front of you is only a prop. But when you reach that mental level, you can ignore the eye consciousness and focus on what is there in your mind.

106

He told the student to close her eyes and focus on the mental image. As she did, the line drifted up again. He told the student she could get better with practice. He understands that scientifically when one is focused, there are more neurons connected in the brain. The Dalai Lama argues that we need to take the time to develop peace of mind. This type of mental toughness does not come overnight.

## Reinventing education

The Dalai Lama sees an urge for reinventing education. He believes today's education is lacking in moral education, ethics, and what he calls, 'the oneness of humanity'[3]—essentially our quest for happiness. Education is the tool with which we can extend our biological instinct for compassion toward our loved ones outward, into the greater world community.

The Dalai Lama argues, "Many students study business and economics with an aim to become rich. So, they work tirelessly, without sufficient sleep, always busy, busy, busy. But there's no compassion in that—it's just for themselves."[4] He says it is in our own interest to help the world. Reinventing how children are educated is a force of good; it is a theme the Dalai Lama's returns to time and time again in every aspect of his vision.

## Social and emotional learning

Victor Chan first met the Dalai Lama in 1972. Since then, he's written two books with the Dalai Lama and founded the *Dalai Lama Center for Peace and Education*. The organization triggered a social movement with social and emotional learning (SEL) in schools throughout British Columbia. SEL has taken on many forms through a plethora of curricula used in schools around the world; it is a movement that teaches life skills such as managing upsets, empathy, and cooperation, in essence, emotional hygiene and compassion.

The Dalai Lama was concerned that teachers had not been trained in SEL, so now the University of British Columbia includes this training in its education programs and also offer a master's degree in the topic. Many might fear the results of this type of education at first, but the Dalai Lama encourages, "You'll see the results. Start with one school, then ten, then

107

one thousand. Here you're implementing a pilot project."[3] Many of the programs extend learning beyond the school days to include community, parents, and activities as well.

### A call to care

This entire chapter has focused on how we can reinvent education to teach the children about compassion. At the Smith College Campus school, fifth-graders in Emily Endris's class sit in a circle and have been given the assignment to observe one classmate and to carefully note what they admire about them. Ms. Endris instructs them to look each other in the eye and to compliment each other. The student who receives the appreciation thanks the one giving it and then they each reflect on how it feels to say something true and complimentary to another – and also to be the one at the receiving end. Powerful!

The verdict?

A lot of smiles and good feelings. The discussion afterward also focuses on the authenticity of the compliments and the fact that when you really pay attention to someone, you see aspects of the person you hadn't noticed before.

These exercises are a part of the R & D lab at Smith College, where teachers in training try out their skills and college students taking courses in child development, come to observe.

More than that, the school also participates in a pilot project called *Call to Care by the Mind and Life Institute*, which happens to be a few miles up the road from Smith College. The Dalai Lama has been mentioning the project in his talks across the country whereby he wants the scientific standards of the programs and research to be impeccable.

The Dalai Lama sees the SEL training and the *Call to Care* as cornerstones of his vision, forces for good. He sees the program and education as part theoretical and part practical applications for life. He believes this education could draw on ancient Indian psychology as well as on recent psychological findings to widen and deepen our understanding of emotion and lay the groundwork for change.

In the end, the Dalai Lama envisions an education that is not just about good minds but about good people. He puts it this way, "Our existing modern education system is oriented toward materialist values. We need an education about inner values to lead a healthy life."[4]

As he continued to speak to the audience at Princeton University, "Keep your high standards of education, but it would be more complete if you also included something about warmheartedness."[6]

To educating the heart,
Dr. Crystal

## Notes

[1] http://www.dalailamaquotes.org/
[2] Daniel Goleman, *A force for good: The Dalai Lama's vision for our world*, (New York, NY: Bantam Books, 2009), 177.
[3] Goleman, *Force for good*, 183.
[4] Goleman, *Force for good*, 183.
[5] Goleman, *Force for good*, 184.
[6] Goleman, *Force for good*, 190.

# 31

# SERVANT LEADERSHIP AND LONG VIEW

*"I feel optimistic about the future because humanity seems to be growing more mature; scientists are paying more attention to our inner values, to the study of mind and the emotions. There is a clear desire for peace and concern for the environment."*

~Dalai Lama[1]

Servant-leaders understand that taking the long view to positive outcomes for the world, is a part of being a force for good. Thinking in new ways is critical to creating a compassionate world. This is what the Dalai Lama argues in the book, *A Force for Good: The Dalai Lama's Vision for Our World,* Chapter Eleven, **The Long View.**[2]

The Dalai Lama's vision for the world seems radically different from the one we know and can seem impossibly idealistic. But, as Baba Amte once said, "No one has the right to arrange a funeral for the future."[3]

In the sense that the servant-leaders guide people toward a shared goal, servant leadership is widely distributed and is demonstrated in all of the stories shared in Goleman's book. Whether we are within our family, among friends, on social media, in an organization, or society as a whole, we are all servant-leaders in one way or another, if only from time to time.

The Dalai Lama argues that we can all play a part in the network of influence and impact in the world today. Indeed, a lot of the changes the Dalai Lama speaks of are systemic, and it will take all of us to make the shift. I wrote about systems thinking some time ago.

The Dalai Lama presented an example of a movement within science to study contemplative practice and how it started with just one scientist. Then, that scientist engaged friends in the conversation, and then they informed and invited other friends to the conversation.

The scientist met colleagues at conferences and all of a sudden, an informal network formed into an active professional network that collectively came together to find solutions.

"No single person can change the world. Now, we are in the modern era, with democracy, it's really the voice of the people together, the collective, that will make the difference" says the Dalai Lama.[4]

But what about the discouragement many feel, Goleman asked the Dalai Lama. He said that we should plants the seeds of a better world. We have to begin somewhere and know that shift is gradual. Education and awareness are critical for the younger generation.[5]

At the end of the day, we should not be daunted by these lofty goals. The Dalai Lama says about his own efforts, I am not expecting to see a result. It may take twenty or thirty years or more. I tell students in their twenties that they may live to see the results, but we all have a responsibility to act now, even if we will never see the fruition of our efforts.[6]

Servant-leaders understand that thinking for the long term, that is to have a **long view**, helps us to leave the world a better place for our children than as we found it.

To the long view,
Dr. Crystal.

## Notes

[1] http://www.dalailamaquotes.org/
[2] Daniel Goleman, *A force for good: The Dalai Lama's vision for our world*, (New York, NY: Bantam Books, 2009), 193.
[3] Goleman, *Force for good*, 202.
[4] Goleman, *Force for good*, 206.
[5] Goleman, *Force for good*, 207.
[6] Goleman, *Force for good*, 208.

## 32

## ACT NOW

Today's blog will complete our series on compassion using Daniel Goleman's book, *A Force for Good: The Dalai Lama's Vision for Our World.*

Servant-leaders understand that action speaks louder than words. In this sense, compassion is expressed in many ways and the desire to do something that is, act now, as a force for good is what the Dalai Lama argues in the book, *A Force for Good: The Dalai Lama's Vision for Our World* (2015), by Daniel Goleman in the final chapter, Chapter Twelve, **Act Now**.[1]

The message the Dalai Lama has shared with us is two-fold; taking control of our destructive emotions rather than acting on them and acting on our concern for the well-being of others from the sense of the oneness of humanity. The Dalai Lama's vision is one that suggests the *what* and *how* of compassion, but his core lesson to us is also that we should cultivate a warm heart and foster human values. We must act now and persist to do so. We should act even if the cause seems hopeless, and never give up.

The Dalai Lama's vision for shifting our consciousness and our social reality begins inside each of us. We can start with ourselves and then help transform our society person by person or project by project. The Dalai Lama argues, "Start with yourself, but don't stop there. Act for others, with positivity."[2] Our efforts should be voluntary, knowing that we can accelerate the transformation of our society by transforming ourselves first.

Each one of us can transform by shifting our emotional center to become better vessels for compassion.

And to help that, we can revamp education to include tools for this inner shift for the younger generation.

## Take it to scale

Activism is the key for people who are a force for good. Dekila Chungyalpa, the McCluskey Fellow at the Yale School of Forestry and Environmental Studies, puts it this way, "Almost every activist I know is actually an optimist at heart. You really have to believe that the society will be better off. I think there is a natural ebullience, an enthusiasm that comes from inside. We're convinced, no matter what the odds are, that we will win."[3]

The Dalai Lama advises us to think and go *big*. Spreading the good you do as far as possible is the key. If we embark on some good work (like the community work that I have been doing for the last six weeks or more), we should do it well and with maximal impact.

In short, go to scale.

And sometimes when we consider the enormity of the challenge, we may feel like throwing in the towel, giving up. But, we must remember that each act that we do, no matter how simple or insignificant it may seem, when it is multiplied by others (10,000 or 1 million of us) we can have an enormous impact.

## The human connection

The Dalai Lama believes the pathway from thought to action is through making a commitment to other people. We must work with one another, commit to one another, and act with one another.

Indeed, compassionate acts are contagious. Thomas Jefferson coined it as 'moral elevation,' the sort of inspiration we feel to help when we witness random acts of kindness.[4] Many psychologists have verified this feeling through a plethora of studies, but we all know the feeling.

## Think, plan, act

The Dalai Lama believes far more in the power of individuals to make an impact over huge top-down changes, whether from an organization or from the government. And, he believes that you can't force people to be compassionate. His call to action for us is to not wait for society to change.

113

We can start now, wherever we are. "Everyone can find a context in which they can make a difference. The human community is nothing, but individuals combined," says the Dalai Lama.[5]

At the end of the day, the Dalai Lama's vision, Daniel Goleman's book, and this blog have one core point: Seize the opportunity, *now.*

As Servant-leaders, we are a Force for Good.

All is Well. We are Complete. And So It Is.

To acting now,

Dr. Crystal

## Notes

[1] Daniel Goleman, *A force for good: The Dalai Lama's vision for our world*, (New York, NY: Bantam Books, 2009), 209.

[2] Goleman, *Force for good*, 213.

[3] Goleman, *Force for good*, 213.

[4] Goleman, *Force for good*, 217.

[5] Goleman, *Force for good*, 219.

# AUTHENTIC CONVERSATIONS: MOVING FROM MANIPULATION TO TRUTH AND COMMITMENT
by Jamie Showkeir and Maren Showkeir

*Crystal J. Davis*

## 33

# SERVANT LEADERSHIP AND AUTHENTIC CONVERSATIONS

*"It is a shame that so many leaders spend their time pondering their right as leaders instead of their awesome responsibilities as leaders."*

~ James C. Hunter[1]

This week, the blog centers on the lessons found in *Authentic Conversations: Moving from Manipulation to Truth and Commitment* by Jamie Showkeir and Maren Showkeir.[2]

This book is a fascinating read and I hope you will glean valuable insight to use in your work and personal lives. Now, let's get to it…

The premise that many work environments possess the culture of a parent-child mindset is born out of an organization's desire to maintain *control, consistency, and predictability* as a strategy to manage its employees. However, today's fast-paced global arena demands that organizations value *diversity, flexibility, and innovation*.

This philosophy was proposed by Frederick Taylor (who was also ironically named the Father of Scientific Management Theory); it was based on the cynical view that people had to be constantly watched for work to get done.

Since the Industrial Revolution, organizations have been centered on the idea that adults won't choose accountability on their own, so they have to be bribed and coerced into taking responsibility.

Things have to change. Such a shift requires a new conversation. This shift requires an authentic conversation.

117

To begin a new conversation, servant-leaders know that much has been said about the notion of deeply entrenched parent-child cultures (mindsets) in the context of organizations and workplace. Such is the case for many organizations.

What I mean by parent-child cultures is the conversational roles used routinely in organizations that establish and reinforce parent-child cultures.

For example, when employees are asked, "What is it like to work here?" and the response is, "This is a difficult place to work. The pace is hectic and demanding. Nothing ever changes, and I feel like all they want me to do is show up and do what they say."

**Or**

Like the video I saw on Facebook this morning where a guy was videotaping a Burger King employee (who make $7.50 an hour) dumping used oil in the sewer drain. When asked why he was doing it, the guy replied, "Hey man, my boss told me to do it. I am just following orders."

These examples point to parent-child like cultures that exist in organizations.

It is critical for organizations to move on from a parent-child culture to an adult-adult culture so that organizations are equipped to survive in this highly technical, global, diverse, and ever-changing world.

The question I ask myself is who do organizations want to show up at work each day? Children, who need a long list of rules and regulations and constant oversight to be held accountable? Or servant-leaders who can, and choose to, hold themselves accountable for the greater good of the organization?

If we are to move from parent-child relationships at work, we have to get a sense of adult-to-adult relationships. There are critical agreements that can be framed as rights and responsibilities. So, in this context, rights are what we **claim**, and responsibility is what we **choose**.

Claiming rights without responsibility is anarchy, and responsibilities without rights is oppression. Both are necessary if organizations are to shift into adult-to-adult relationships. For authentic conversations to begin, I thought about the following notions for organizations:

- employees and leaders must become the eyes and voice of the organization.
- employees and leaders bring an independent point of view and are open to others' perspectives.
- employees and leaders are expected to raise the difficult issues.
- employees and leaders extend a spirit of goodwill in their endeavor.
- employees and leaders create business literacy in others.
- employees and leaders choose accountability for the success of the whole business.
- employees and leaders manage their morale, motivation, and commitment.
- employees and leaders communicate with everyone in every department about everything.

Starting a new conversation can be difficult. Disappointments will occur. But, servant-leaders need not wait for the entire organization to get on board to make this change. Organizations can change the culture at the moment, in any space. So, what would a new conversation in organizations sound like?

- honestly acknowledging the difficult issues and naming the harsh reality.
- state your contribution to the difficult issue and acknowledge its harmful effects.
- state the risks and acknowledge difficulties, including the possibility that things might not work out.
- frame choices about how we can engage the future without referring to the problems of the present.

Of course, to have new conversations that are authentic and transforming, clarity about one's own intention is essential. This requires keen self-awareness and a willingness to be honest and vulnerable. Personal transformation comes first. It is the most important work of an emerging servant-leader.

To authentic conversations,
Dr. Crystal

## Notes

[1] http://www.azquotes.com/quote/1035177

[2] J. Showkeir and M. Showkeir, *Authentic conversations: Moving from manipulation to truth and Commitment*, (San Francisco, CA: Berrett-Koehler Publishers, Inc., 2008).

[3] Showkeir and Showkeir, *Authentic conversations*, 8.

*Crystal J. Davis*

## START WITH HUMILITY: LESSONS FROM AMERICA'S QUIET CEO'S ON HOW TO BUILD TRUST AND INSPIRE FOLLOWERS
by Merwyn Hayes and Michael Comer

*Crystal J. Davis*

## 34

## SERVANT LEADERSHIP: CONFIDENCE, AND CRUCIBLE MOMENTS

I have recently enrolled in a certification class with the Greenleaf Center for Servant Leadership, Key Practices of Servant Leadership 2.0. Our first book, *Start with Humility: Lessons from America's Quiet CEO's on How to Build Trust and Inspire Followers* by Merwyn Hayes and Michael Comer, is fascinating![1] The reading centers on humility and leadership, highlighting five CEOs who have demonstrated this quality in their years of leadership. What is interesting is how these leaders keep humility at the forefront of their being, how they work with others and how they work through challenges.

Our first discussion question asked, "What do you think about the dynamic of humility and confidence?" Chapter Seven of the book entitled, *Check Your Ego at the Door*, highlights Jim Thompson, Former CEO of the Federation of State Medical Boards.[2] His talks about his crucible moment (a crucible moment is a humbling moment; crucible moments are transformational experiences that often define a person's worldview or philosophy), and how he used his crucible moment to transcend an overwhelming and ruinous situation to become an even more effective and humble leader.

When I started thinking about my leadership, confidence, humility, and crucible moments, one came to mind immediately.

I had a boss, several years ago, who was threatened by everything that I did. He hired me to administer a grant. It was a rather huge grant and pretty quickly, I found that he micromanaged every aspect of the daily operations (my job). I did not know how to approach him. I was going home frustrated, every day. I wanted to quit.

Then, a few months into the job, we attended a conference together. At the conference, after a workshop, it was near dinner time and so I asked him to dinner. He seemed to be put off by my invite. I don't think anyone (a subordinate) ever asked him to join in something other than work. He did not give off the type of friendliness where you would want to hang out with him after work. He was not humble, and he acted and conducted himself in an arrogant manner. But he accepted. We had small talk about the conference and other things. Then I said to him, "Dr. Doe, what is your philosophy?" He looked puzzled. I don't think anyone ever asked him about his personal perspective on the work we were doing.

Starting there, our conversation lasted more than two hours. I told him about my own worldview and how it had an impact on my work. He told me his. In the end, I gained insight in regard to the person and leader he was and he about me. It seemed he left the conversation impressed.

I was humble, yet confident. I assured him about my level of commitment and loyalty to the grant and the kids we served. I let him know (in a compassionate way) that I did not need to be micromanaged. My best work would come when I was allowed to own my work, be responsible for it and flow in my way...and in my style. From that point on, we worked better together...for as much as we could.

Change is slow and painful. I left the grant after one year. But, I felt fully confident that I had done my best job. So, I left feeling good. You know what? It was years later that I was working on another unrelated grant for a church.

They invited Dr. Doe to the meeting to ask about including the school district in the grant. There we were together again. In the humblest way I had ever heard him, he said to the administrators, "Crystal worked with our grant several years ago, and she did an outstanding job. You guys have a good person here. She does exemplary work." Wow! I almost fell off my chair! Was this the same individual?

In the end, it does matter how bosses treat their employees. As I began supervising people, I always remembered this experience (crucible moment). In my leadership evolvement, I emulate Jim Thompson in our book; have genuine respect for everyone (bottom to top), let people do their jobs, care about the people who work for you, and exemplify humility. These qualities should not be mistaken for weaknesses in leadership. I can be tough as nails when needed!

Jo Miller, on her website, **BeLeaderly.com** says that there are three weird tips for increasing your influence. I think they align loosely with our discussion; wake up to a power pose, be an energizer, and use the most powerful word in the English Language.

Do you have a crucible moment? Think about it. Journal about it. And then, wake up each morning to your power pose…with humility.

To crucible moments,
Dr. Crystal

### Notes

1 M. A. Hayes and M.D. Comer, Start with humility: Lessons from America's quiet CEO's on how to build trust and inspire followers. (Westfield, IN: Greenleaf Center for Servant Leadership, 2010).
2 Hayes and Comer Start with humility, 75.

## 35

## THE YEAR OF SERVANT LEADERSHIP IN REVIEW - 2015

*"Great leaders start within."*

~David Berry[1]

It has been an amazing year for my learning blog, **Lead.From.Within**. Who knew the journey would yield great learning experiences (and yet more to come), allow me to network with many great leaders, and get my message across to leaders in 38 countries? Wow, for a person who just started learning how to blog, that's mind blowing!

I've read a few blogs and five key messages (questions) resonate with me that I'd like to share with you; but first, let's take a quick glance at what we've already learned and the tools we've gained for our servant leadership tool box:

**Five books that have inspired me:**

1. *Seven Pillars of Servant Leadership* by James Sipe and Don Frick
2. *The Speed of Trust: The One Thing That Changes Everything* by Stephen M. Covey
3. *A Force for Good: The Dalai Lama's Vision for Our World* by Daniel Goleman
4. *Authentic Conversations: Moving from Manipulations to Truth and Commitment* by Jamie Showkeir and Maren Showkeir
5. *Start with Humility: Lessons from America's Quiet CEO's on how to build trust and inspire followers* by Hayes & Comer

**Themes touched upon:**

1. Lessons on *humility* as servant-leaders
2. Seven Pillars of servant leadership (Character, puts people first, skilled communicator, compassionate collaborator, has foresight, systems thinker, moral authority)
3. The value of real authentic conversation at work that lead away from parent-child like conversations to adult conversations and consciousness.
4. The five waves of trust (self-trust, relationship trust, organizational trust, market trust, and societal trust)
5. Trust (13 Behaviors and the Four Cores)
6. Compassion (A Force for Good)

Two bloggers that challenged me to greater depths of service and spirituality are David Berry (https://rule13learning.com/) and Gregory Toole (https://somseva.org/blog/). If you have a chance, you too could refer to them.

Servant-leaders understand that to serve others, one must be open to learning and to ever emerging as a leader who serves.

*"What is it you believe you do that makes a difference to other people and to mankind?"*

Clifton and Nelson[2]

As time goes by, I will continue to ask myself the following questions to *stay present* with servant leadership and its message;

1. How can I serve?
2. How can you serve?

3. How can we serve together?
4. Under what context am I serving?
5. What do I want the end result of my service to look like?

I wish to thank each one of you whole heartedly for your support of my blog! I am indeed in a debt of gratitude to you. I look forward to the next year with great joy and anticipation for our work together. All is well. We are complete. And so it is. Namaste.

To the year gone by,
Dr. Crystal

## Notes

[1] https://rule13learning.com/blog-2/
[2] Donald O. Clifton and Paula Nelson, *Soar with Your Strengths: A Simple Yet Revolutionary Philosophy of Business and Management* (1992), Intro.vi.

# PRACTICING SERVANT-LEADERSHIP: SUCCEEDING THROUGH TRUST, BRAVERY, AND FORGIVENESS
by Larry C. Spears and Michelle Lawrence

*Crystal J. Davis*

Crystal J. Davis

# 36

# WHO IS A SERVANT LEADER?

We begin our series on servant leadership using the book, *Practicing Servant-Leadership: Succeeding Through Trust, Bravery, and Forgiveness* by Larry C. Spears and Michelle Lawrence, as our guide.[1]

*"Allow the way to your great work to be guided by your service to others."*

~Mollie Marti[2]

Who is a servant-leader? The first chapter delves into this question and provides a short excerpt from Robert K. Greenleaf's seminal essay, *'The Servant as Leader.'* (Greenleaf, 1977) which is essential understanding, definition and philosophy of servant leadership.[3]

Greenleaf presents us with two questions, to which he answers with a resounding 'yes' concerning a servant-leader. He asks, "Servant and Leader-can these two roles be fused in one real person, in all levels of status or calling? And, if so, can that person live and be productive in the real world of the present? The first chapter is an attempt to explain why and to suggest how Greenleaf crystallized his vision of servant leadership through his reading of the novel, *Journey to the East* by Herman Hesse, a work that deeply moved him. In the story, the servant, Leo, was the caring leader. Leo's leadership style was that of a servant such that the people claimed that they did everything themselves.

During the journey, Leo disappeared. The group fell apart and abandoned the spiritual quest. The group realized that they needed Leo. Years later, the narrator found Leo and learned Leo was the head of the noble order, its guiding spirit, and a great leader. The narrator had only known of Leo as a servant. Indeed, a leader who exemplifies servant

131

leadership, such as Leo, can see the effect of his or her leadership through the growth of the people. Who is a servant-leader? A servant-leader serves first, just as Leo was portrayed.

Greenleaf goes on to say that when he came upon Hesse's book in 1958, he had been listening (as always) and searching for voices of prophecy, those who spoke of truth for the benefit of humankind. He knew the message in Hesse's book was of a prophetic nature.

Greenleaf puts it this way,

'I now embrace the theory of prophecy which holds that prophetic voices of great clarity, and with a quality of insight equal to that of any age, are speaking cogently all the time. Men and women of a stature equal to the greatest prophets of the past are now with us, addressing the problems of the day and pointing to a better way to live fully and serenely in these times'.[4]

What is fascinating is that Greenleaf understood that prophetic vision is directly tied to the level of seeking and the responsiveness of the hearers. So, those prophets grow in stature as people respond to their message. Indeed, it is the seekers, then, who make prophets. Isn't that beautiful? Doesn't it give us a perfect example of servant leadership?

Being careful not to ignore the great voices of the past, Greenleaf says that servant-leaders do not wake up each morning with the compulsion to reinvent the wheel, rather if one is a servant-either leader or follower-one is always searching, listening, experiencing a better wheel for the times in the making. It can emerge any day, and anyone of us can discover it from our personal experience.

Servant leadership is positioned to help us today. Greenleaf was hopeful then that despite tension and conflict in the world, there would be more *natural* servant-leaders, such as you and me, to see clearly the world as it is and to listen carefully to the prophetic voices that are speaking now.

Servant-leaders, that is, you and I, are challenging the pervasive injustice with greater force, and we are taking sharper issue with the disparity in the world concerning the quality of society, available resources, and the performance of the institutions that exist to serve society. We see that right now, through the servant-leaders who are stepping forward in service to the recent tragedy in Orlando (CNN, 2016).[5] Indeed, we are helping the world to relate to one another in more supporting and less coercive and hateful ways.

I choose to remain hopeful.

Greenleaf tells us specifically and concretely, "A new moral principle is emerging, which holds that the only authority deserving one's allegiance is that which is freely and knowingly granted by the **led** to the leader, in response to, and in proportion to, the clearly evident servant stature of the leader."[6]

Phew, isn't that powerful? The allegiance of the 'led' is granted to the leader only through and by the evidence of service by that leader.

In the end, Greenleaf believed that Hesse was telling us in his book that Leo was the symbolic personification of Hesse's aspiration to serve through his literary creations-creations that were greater than himself and his work, for which he was but the channel. Thus, Leo and his literary creations would carry on and serve and lead in a way that he, a twisted and tormented man, could not.

Isn't that the dilemma for us all as servant-leaders? As we create, and as we emerge as servant-leaders, we cannot project ourselves beyond ourselves to serve and lead.

Servant leadership is not a popular concept. It is still painstakingly making its way into the mainstream of leadership concepts today. Greenleaf reminds us that the danger, perhaps is to hear the analyst too much and the artist too little.

At the end of the day, I agree with Greenleaf, that Albert Camus was one of the great artists of his time and deserves the title of prophet. I have posted the last paragraph of Camus's published lecture, entitled *'Create Dangerously'* (Camus, 1957)[7] many times on my Facebook page. It reminds me daily of my vision, my mission as a servant-leader, and the reason why my circle of influence continues to emerge as servant-leaders by my modeling and example of service.

'One may long, as I do, for a gentler flame, a respite, a pause for musing. But perhaps there is no other peace for the artist than what she finds in the heat of combat. "Every wall is a door," Emerson correctly said. Let us not look for the door, and the way out, anywhere but in the wall against which we are living. Instead, let us seek the respite where it is—in the very thick of battle. For in my opinion, and this is where I shall close, it is there. Great ideas, it has been said, come into the world as gently as doves. Perhaps, then, if we listen attentively, we shall hear, amid the uproar of empire and nations, a faint flutter of wings, the gentle stirring of life and hope. Some will say that this hope lies in a nation, others, in a man. I believe rather that it is awakened, revived, nourished by millions of solitary individuals whose deeds and works every day negate frontiers and the crudest implications of history. As a result, there shines forth fleetingly the ever-threatened truth that each and every woman, on the foundations of her own sufferings and joys, builds for them all."[8]

To creating dangerously,
Dr. Crystal

## Notes

[1] L. C. Spears and M. Lawrence, *Practicing Servant Leadership: Succeeding through trust, bravery, and forgiveness*, (San Francisco, CA: Jossey-Bass, 2004).
[2] https://www.goodreads.com/quotes/558840-allow-the-way-to-your-great-work-to-be-guided
[3] R. K. Greenleaf, *The servant as leader*, (Indianapolis, IN: The Robert K. Greenleaf Center, 1970), 1.
[4] Greenleaf, *Servant as Leader*, 2
[5] http://www.cnn.com/2016/06/12/us/orlando-nightclub-shooting/index.html
[6] Greenleaf, *Servant as Leader*, 3
[7] Spears and Lawrence, *Practicing Servant Leadership*, 5 – 6.
[8] Spears and Lawrence, *Practicing Servant Leadership*, 5 – 6.

## 37

# SIX APPLICATIONS OF SERVANT LEADERSHIP

*"Servant Leadership deals with the reality of power in everyday life—its legitimacy, the ethical restraints upon it and the beneficial results that can be attained through the appropriate use of power."*

~New York Times[1]

*The Understanding and Practice of Servant-Leadership* by Larry C. Spears is Chapter Two of the book we are using as a guide, *Practicing Servant-Leadership: Succeeding Through Trust, Bravery, and Forgiveness* by Larry C. Spears and Michelle Lawrence.[2]

The concept of servant leadership has continued to explode onto the organizational and corporate scene since my enlightenment of the concept from an academic (although lifelong) perspective six years ago. In fact, we have witnessed this explosion on and interest in servant leadership with fire over the last fifteen years. A concept coined by Robert Greenleaf now over 40 years ago, is creating a quiet revolution in today's workplace all over the world.

Servant leadership is about a **shift in consciousness** about the way we live and work. It is about working, based on teamwork and collective decision-making. It is based in an ethical and caring concern for others, and it is about enhancing the growth of others while caring about the quality of our institutions and organizations. Indeed, servant leadership is a better, more holistic approach to serving others first. Others meaning employees, customers, and the communities in which we live.

We are not naïve in thinking that servant leadership is a quick fix to the problems in life and at the workplace. Servant-leaders understand that this way of **being** is a long-term, every-single-day, transformational approach to life and work. And so, we as servant-leaders live each day in a conscious effort to create positive change for our immediate world (our job, our home, our kids, our community) and that trickles out into the greater world community.

My mom is a servant-leader. Granted, she didn't know about Robert Greenleaf or the other great scholars of today such as DePree, Senge, Covey, Wheatley, Autry, and many other popular writers who teach servant leadership. She just worked in the church, in her family, at her job, and in her community as servant-leader. I saw first-hand as a child how she worked first as a cook at our local county jail preparing food for the inmates. After 30 years, promoted to the Food Service Director, she showed great care and concern for the preparation of the food for the inmates of the jail. She abhorred people's opinions that prisoners should be glad that they can even eat. She fried her famous chicken and would sneak some to the prisoners; even the jailers would come up to the kitchen and beg for a piece. Although a stern woman, she had a heart of gold and the prisoners knew it.

They felt it.

It was the same way with her work in the church. I have lost count of the number of church dinners that I helped in cooking and preparing. They knew my mom would present and serve the food to the people with the utmost professionalism, love, and care. And everyone loved my mom's cooking.

I was reminded of this childhood experience as I was reading Juana Bordas article, *Pluralistic Reflections on Servant Leadership* (Greenleaf Center for Servant Leadership, 1998) where she said, "Many women, minorities and people of color have long traditions of servant leadership in their cultures. Servant leadership has very old roots in many of the indigenous cultures - cultures that were holistic, cooperative, communal, intuitive, and spiritual.[3] These cultures centered on being guardians of the future and respecting the ancestors who walked before."[3]

This was my mother's life. This is what she taught by example.

And today, I have the ideal opportunity to practice my servant leadership through my taking care of her for the last 16 years. She now lives the rest of her autumn days in a nursing home, most days remembering her life. She is proud, and I am grateful that she showed me the way. She is excited that I took an academic path toward understanding and teaching servant leadership. But, at the end of the day, she would tell you, just *be* it!

So, Spears provides us with a glimpse into the six applications of servant leadership that are being used by organizations across the country today. Here is a short recap of each.

**Servant-leadership as an institutional model**

As an institutional model, servant leadership advocates a group-oriented approach to decision-making and seeks consensus over the old top-down form of leadership. Many organizations today use the servant leadership model as a guiding philosophy. Southwest Airlines, Starbucks, and the Men's Wearhouse, are just a few names of such organizations.

**Education and training of nonprofit trustees**

Greenleaf wrote extensively on the role of boards of directors within institutions and the theoretical and ethical basis for their service. His essay, 'Trustees as Servants' asked two pivotal questions of Boards and Trustees, "Whom do you serve?" and "For what purpose?" Greenleaf argued that boards must a make a radical shift in how they approach their roles so as to create institutions of great depth and quality.

**Community leadership programs**

The third application of servant leadership is its role in community leadership organizations and the importance of building a true community. M. Scott Peck wrote about this in his book, *A World Waiting to be Born*, in which he says, "The world will be saved if we can create three well-managed, large institutions—one in the private sector, one in the public sector, and one in the nonprofit sector. I know that such excellence in management will be achieved through an organizational culture of civility routinely utilizing the mode of community."[4]

## Service-learning programs

A fourth application of servant leadership is the use of service-learning in the various colleges and universities across the country. During the last twenty-five years, experiential learning education programs are developed in virtually every college, university, and secondary schools. Service-learning has become a major focus, combining service and learning. *The National Society for Experiential Education* has published a massive three-volume work on the topic.

## Leadership education

A fifth application of servant leadership is the use of the philosophy in formal and informal, as well as in corporate education and training programs. Dozens of management, organizational, and leadership consultants employ servant leadership materials as a part of their work with organizations. As a part of total quality management approaches, servant leadership is making headway for corporations in understanding how business is developed and conducted, while still positively affecting the bottom line.

## Personal transformation

Programs relating to personal growth and transformation are using the servant leadership approach as a way for people to grow and evolve spiritually, professionally, emotionally, and intellectually. Servant leadership has ties to emotional intelligence and human potential. The key to servant leadership is that it offers and encourages everyone to seek out opportunities to both serve and lead.

In the end, servant leadership is full of curious and meaningful paradoxes, just like life. The seeds of servant leadership have been planted in the minds and hearts of people who seek to better the human condition. Indeed, servant leadership provides the vehicle and framework for known and unknown individuals to continue to hope and guide the way to the creation of a better, more conscious and caring world community.

To a better world,
Dr. Crystal

## Notes

1 L. C. Spears and M. Lawrence, *Practicing Servant Leadership: Succeeding through trust, bravery, and forgiveness*, (San Francisco, CA: Jossey-Bass, 2004), 9.
2 Spears and Lawrence, *Practicing Servant Leadership*, 9.
3 https://www.regent.edu/acad/global/publications/sl_proceedings/2005/spears_practic e.pdf
4 M. Scott Peck, *A World Waiting to be Born: Civility Rediscovered*, (New York, NY: Bantam books, 1994).

38

# FOUR WAYS BOARDS OF DIRECTORS USE SERVANT LEADERSHIP

*"The Board Chairperson is like the moon shining by a light no less spectacular because it is only reflected. This kind of chair never forgets that the conductor doesn't make the music."*

~John Carver[1]

*The Unique Double Servant-Leadership Role of the Board Chairperson* by John Carver is Chapter Three of the book we are using as a guide, *Practicing Servant-Leadership: Succeeding Through Trust, Bravery, and Forgiveness* by Larry C. Spears and Michelle Lawrence.[2]

John Carver provides an excellent discussion and a sort of paradigm shift on the role of the board chairperson and the role of the board as a group in his chapter on servant leadership. Having served on several boards of directors in the past, I am always refreshed by Carver's no-nonsense concepts for boards and their chairs, and how eloquently and transparently servant leadership serves as the way for boards to operate to better serve the people and the organization.

Carver argued that boards of directors are in trouble and have been in trouble for years. He quotes Peter Drucker (1974), Harold Geneen (1984) and the Danforth Foundation report in 1992, indicating that boards are primarily non-functioning. Geneen (1984) said that about 95% of the top 500 companies of America's boards are not doing what they are supposed to do-morally, ethically, and legally.

And that they couldn't, even if they wanted to.

In this vein, Carver proposes four ways that boards can shift in consciousness to become a functioning board. Here is a recap of each.

## Transformation toward a substantially new institution

Carver created a program called the Policy Governance® model which sets a new course for board leadership that aligns with Robert Greenleaf's vision to, "invite people to consider a new domain of leadership grounded in a state of being, not doing."[3] Servant-leaders understand that leadership and service are not something you perform, rather it is an expression of being. Transforming toward a new institution is not about organizing a better agenda or about more fundraising. It is about a deeper level of consciousness whereby leadership at a high-level concern itself with values-the importance of life, commitment to life-and the trade-offs of a life of service.

Governing boards have to be able to combine the ideas of technology and values to connect, as Carver says, who we are and what we can do. The compelling question that John Gardner asks us as servant-leaders is, "Do we have it in us to create a future worthy of our past?"[4] Board leadership must integrally mean the phrase, 'on behalf of'; this holds true for every single motion, vote, idea, action, and plan where the leader must act on behalf of others. Indeed, the best of board governance is possible when it includes the concepts of servant leadership.

## Where servanthood begins: Fidelity to the organization

Board leadership are invited to operate under the awareness that it is to be *owner-representative*. This means that the board understands that if they are operating on someone's behalf, they should know who that someone *is*. And that the board's role consists of an intimate relationship with those owners, not its relationship to the staff. Carver argues that the board is a servant to the owners. In this way, the board takes it upon itself to know what the owners want before it decides on what the organizational goals should be. The owners should expect that a board operating on their behalf knows about them, better than they know about themselves, regarding the organization and the matters at hand. What a Texas legislator once said, sums it up, "I vote the way my constituents would vote if they knew what I know."[4]

## The discipline of leadership

Carver discusses the concept called the *problem of agency* which is defined as using one's own judgment on behalf of someone else. The challenge with the problem of agency is that an agent has to be able to subjugate their personal needs in the service of the other. This is what servant leadership is about.

Board members who are servant-leaders know that when they take their seats, a transformation must take place wherein they are the vessels through which others dream, decide, envision, and intend. De Tocqueville's experiences capture this point beautifully. Citizens, he said, got involved in their local civic organizations first out of self-interest; yet as they became keenly aware and mindful of their public responsibility, they began to transcend their self-interest to the interest of others. This is the transformation board members must engage in as servant-leaders.

Another crucial point for board members to remember is that as servant-leaders, board members must make the transition from an operational mindset to a governing mindset. To not make this transition will cripple the board. Operational behavior does not serve the board of directors, rather a conceptual mindset is what is needed. Greenleaf referenced this when he said, "Leadership, in the sense of going out ahead to show the way is more conceptual than operating."[5] It is necessary for board members to become conceptual people who envision a world that *isn't*, rather than think and operate from a world that *is*.

I have been on boards where it was our goal to recruit members with a certain skill set, say, for example, an attorney, an accountant, etc. to make sure we would have the skills that we needed on the board. But, that can work against a board. Carver says that the board should learn to use experts to inform the wisdom of the board, but never to substitute for it. Wow! Boards are invited to take responsibility as a group and not lean on one skill set to save itself from its group responsibility. There is a huge difference in board-as-expert-collection from the board-as-responsible servant-leaders for an ownership.

## From responsible individuals to responsible boards

Lastly, Carver points out that it is not enough for trustees to be servant-leaders, individually. Doing so is not conducive to creating a servant leadership group. He says that boards can easily be incompetent groups of competent people, untrustworthy groups of trustworthy people, and cruel groups of good-hearted people.

Bam! I had to read that twice!

Greenleaf reminded us that the role of servant-leaders as board members is to act as a *unitary* body.[6] It is all about working as a group. Carver says there is a simple way to test this. He says that any board that authentically works as a group, will tell its CEO, "When we speak as individuals in or out of board meetings, you never have to pay attention to any of us!" Working as a group of members, allows boards to delegate clearly and powerfully to a CEO. As Carver pointed out, board members must speak with one voice and one voice only. A chairperson's authority must come from a group decision. This is not to say or imply that there will always be unanimous votes, but that if the mindset and consciousness are not spoken as a group, it hasn't spoken at all.

Carver pulls us on the carpet as board members regarding our consciousness and ways of working for the organization and the owners. He uses servant leadership as a guidepost for how we can radically shift the way we see our role as board members. With my current role as a board member of a state coalition, these concepts and ideas are here to remind me of my goal as a servant-leader with this board.

Caroline Myss, in her book, *Invisible Acts of Power: Channeling Grace in your Everyday Life* puts it this way, "We must come to terms with our personal agendas and desires while on the path of impersonal, spiritual service. Our task is to infuse our action with all our faith and belief in its goodness and release it into the universe to do its invisible work."[7]

To boards that serve,

Dr. Crystal

## Notes

[1] L. C.S pears and M. Lawrence, *Practicing Servant Leadership: Succeeding through trust, bravery, and forgiveness*, (San Francisco, CA: Jossey-Bass, 2004), 46.

[2] Spears and Lawrence, *Practicing Servant* Leadership, 25.

[3] R. K. Greenleaf, *Trustees as Servants*, (Indianapolis, IN: The Greenleaf Center for Servant Leadership, 1994), 27.

[4] Spears and Lawrence, *Practicing Servant* Leadership, 32.

[5] Spears and Lawrence, *Practicing Servant* Leadership, 35.

[6] Spears and Lawrence, *Practicing Servant* Leadership, 37.

[7] S. C. Myss, *Invisible acts of power: Channeling grace in your everyday life*, (New York, NY: Atria Paperback, 2004), 5.

39

## SIX QUALITIES OF A BOARD CHAIR
## AS SERVANT-LEADER

*"The chair is the servant-leader of the board. The board is servant-leader of the ownership. The chair is, therefore, servant-leader of the servant-leaders."*

~John Carver[1]

*The Unique Double Servant-Leadership Role of the Board Chairperson* by John Carver is Chapter Three of the book we are using as a guide, *Practicing Servant-Leadership: Succeeding Through Trust, Bravery, and Forgiveness* by Larry C. Spears and Michelle Lawrence.[2] Last week, we discussed the role of the members of a board of directors. Since this chapter was full of useful information, I will discuss the end of the chapter today.

Carver argues that a common mistake of boards of directors today is that it looks up to the CEO to tell it what to do. Ask any board today where its last agenda for the meeting came from, and you will find that it is generally the CEO or the Executive Director.

I served as the Executive Director of a nonprofit community-based organization a few years ago, and I will tell you how I managed the board of directors. I had written and won several grants for the organization (that it was building from ground zero) and I helped to recruit the board of directors. Although well-meaning people, they had no idea of how to create or run a board. I found that I was creating and reporting to the board!

That experience reminds me of the Geico commercial where elderly ladies are sitting in the front room and one of the ladies is showing the other two her Facebook timeline which she had created on her front room wall. One of the ladies says, "That's not how any of this works!"

At any rate, there should be a distinction between the line of the CEO and the board chairperson. Most board chairs will not like what Carver says because he says that the board chairperson is staff (the board chairperson is staff to the board), while the CEO is line. The board chairperson is staff to the board just as the finance officer is staff to the CEO. The board chairperson's role, as important as it is, can have no real authority over line personnel, which includes the CEO and the other employees of the organization.

The chairperson's obligation and authority can only derive from a group decision and group expectations. I discussed this 'one voice' approach last week. Remember this does not imply unanimous votes. What it implies is that without a group mindset, the board lacks discipline and until the board exercises a group decision-making power, it has absolutely no authority over anyone.

Carver believes that this type of discipline for a board is difficult to achieve given the current consciousness of how boards operate. And so, the vacuum is filled with uncoordinated individual actions, or worse, the board settles into the 'indolent' comfort of letting someone else just tell them what to do. Sometimes that person is the board chair, but most often that person is the CEO. Boy, do I remember that! It's just the way we've always done it.

A powerful thought from John Carver is this, "governance can only have the needed integrity when boards, not their CEO's assume responsibility for governance."[3] He says it would be a breath of fresh air if board meetings truly became the board's meetings, not the CEO's meetings for the board.

Wow, he stepped on some toes with that statement!

Carver quotes a greeting card that sums up a chair's responsibility, "a friend is someone who learns the words of your song, then sings them back to you when you forget."[4] In this way, the board chair can be encouraging, inspiring, challenging, enlightening, and even cajoling—all within the servant leadership consciousness that call for this kind of tough-love leadership. This kind of tough-love leadership does not let the board members off the hook, though. Group responsibility is tricky and something we are not used to it as boards. We must have the discipline to engage in group responsibility for governance.

The deal is that there is an irony in that the group charges and empowers one of its own to help it be true to itself and its self-defined responsibility. Your experience and mine on the board-the tone of interpersonal exchange, the board's relationship to staff, and the board's relationship to ownership-make a huge difference in board effectiveness, right?

The irony is this: the more the board embraces group responsibility and expresses this through a coherent governance model, the less it matters who the board chair is. It is like that quote from Lao Tzu, "A leader is best when people barely know he exists, when his work is done, his aim fulfilled, they will say: we did it ourselves."[5]

So, how does a board chair garner the discipline to guide a board to group responsibility? What are the core characteristics of a board chairperson who can carry out such a responsibility? I am glad you asked! Carver provides us with six characteristics. And they all align with servant leadership. I will give a re-cap of each below.

**Personal integrity**
The board chairperson must deal, in a straightforward manner, with the trustee relationships and commitments from a place of authenticity. This means no playing favorites and not engaging in games. The board chair's behavior is guided by principles and not politics.

**Ability to leave the CEO alone**
A board chair must have no need to interfere with the CEO's responsibility. While a chair's intervention between the board and its CEO can ease the board member's anxiety in the short term, it can inevitably damage the proper board-CEO relationship.

**Intelligence and conceptual flexibility**
Board members must have the ability to think conceptually. At this level of leadership, the ability to deal with concepts, constructs, and principles is critical to the success of a servant- leader who serves as a board chairperson.

## Mindfulness of group process

A board chairperson must not live and operate naively, unaware of interpersonal and political realities. Rather, a good candidate should be comfortable with group processes and should have the ability to capitalize on the group's skills and talents. More than that, a board chair should operate in a calm and cool manner when the group process goes awry.

## A disposition of servanthood

A good chairperson is a servant-leader who never forgets on whose behalf he or she works and by whose grace he or she exercises authority. This is the most important characteristic. Personally speaking, I would say that a board chair works for the people!

## Ability to confront and lead

A board chair must be able to lead with authority and confront the board members and group with their or its own behavior. A good candidate must be able to say, "We committed ourselves to X yet, we, at this moment, are doing Y. We must either stop or change our commitment. Which shall it be?"

Servant-leaders who serve as board chairpersons understand that these characteristics are ones that allow the leader to lead *modestly in command*. This is the way of a servant-leader. A board chair's role is both compassionate and compelling. It requires self-discipline as it is asking others to do the same.

At the end of the day, this is what Greenleaf has always challenged us to *be* as servant-leaders; the most morally justifiable leaders and leadership are founded in, legitimated by, and yes, even sanctified by servanthood.

This kind of chair never forgets that the conductor does not make the music.

To board chairpersons,
Dr. Crystal

# Notes

[1] L. C. Spears and M. Lawrence, *Practicing Servant Leadership: Succeeding through trust, bravery, and forgiveness,* (San Francisco, CA: Jossey-Bass, 2004), 46.

[2] Spears and Lawrence, *Practicing Servant* Leadership, 25.

[3] Spears and Lawrence, *Practicing Servant* Leadership, 41.

[4] Spears and Lawrence, *Practicing Servant* Leadership, 43.

[5] https://www.brainyquote.com/quotes/lao_tzu_121709

**40**

# THREE QUESTIONS TO CONSIDER AS
# A SERVANT-LEADER

*"Any time people want to focus on my work, servant-leadership, or other values as a way to get better results it's critical to start from the right place. You sincerely have to start with what you yourself are wanting to become, the being and becoming of you."*

~James Autry[1]

*Love and Work* by James Autry represents Chapter Four of the book we are using as a guide, *Practicing Servant-Leadership: Succeeding Through Trust, Bravery, and Forgiveness* by Larry C. Spears and Michelle Lawrence.[2]

In this chapter, we get a glimpse into James Autry's perspective on servant leadership, love, and work through an interview he had had with the then president and CEO of The Greenleaf Center for Servant Leadership, Larry Spears, and John Noble, the then director of the Greenleaf Centre-United Kingdom.

After 28 years in the management field, Autry provides us with real insight into what he has learned about what makes a servant-leader and what makes a great workplace. The interview included many questions. I chose three that resonated with me and hopefully they will resonate with you. Here is a recap of each.

**What are the markers in your life, the people, and events that have helped shape your thinking?**
Autry believes that everything is connected and interrelated. That is, every experience, and every relationship are connected and they all point in the same direction. He said that he learned later in his business career that the most effective managers were those who were thought of as the weakest by

the higher management. He says he tried to manage from the old hierarchal attitudes and it just did not work for him.

The beginning of his transformation happened when he heard a speech by Bob Burnett, the CEO of the Meredith Corporation. Burnett claimed that "the most important thing is love," and this statement forever changed Autry's perspective of leadership in the corporate world. Indeed, he had never heard of managers and CEOs using the word *love* in the business world. So, Autry let go of his old ways of managing and over time saw improvement. Autry argues that when he shifted his consciousness and started supporting people and building a community within the workplace, the company went from 160 million in revenues to 500 million!

**What does servant leadership mean to you?**
Autry hardly ever uses the term 'servant leadership', rather he pairs it with terms such as *being useful* and *being a resource*. He believes that a leader's responsibility is to provide the resources necessary for the team to accomplish their objectives and he understands that the principal resource of the people is *you*, the leader. The leader must serve the people. He says there are five precepts that he lives by; project authenticity and vulnerability, be present, be accepting, see your role as being useful, and be a servant.

Wow!

If every CEO, manager, and employee saw themselves as caring and serving to one another, the corporate world would be different and the profit we so want to make would show up in the bottom line. Every. Single. Time.

**What is your sense of how a leader gets better at developing a servant's heart, and how to view oneself as a servant to others?**
This is the most powerful question asked. Autry's response was, "To me, the road to servanthood has to be almost by definition, a road away from ego. We could shift this over to Buddhism and *say path of heart*-the move to a servant's heart is a move away from ego. I think it has to be done in the context of one's own spiritual development, spiritual growth, and by reading other spiritual disciplines, and picking people you think are spiritual

heroes, those who emulate how you would like to be and following these models, letting them be mentors."[3]

One such person for me, one that I see as a mentor, although I have never met him, is David Berry. I am not exactly sure when I started reading David's blog, but his message instantly struck me as real and authentic, caring and compassionate, spiritual and in-depth. He's a great writer and his message is substantive. You never leave his blog post without a call to action for your own life. Whether that is in your personal life or your professional life as a leader, David always inspires and encourages us to greater and better heights within ourselves. I think he is a servant leader.

His blog this week, *The Story of Self,* perfectly aligns with our discussion here. You should read it and think about your own values, strengths, limitations, and purpose. And then write them down. I did. It's empowering. Servant-leaders understand that this self-work is critical and worth every ounce of effort.

To love and work,
Dr. Crystal

## Notes

[1] L. C. Spears and M. Lawrence, *Practicing Servant Leadership: Succeeding through trust, bravery, and forgiveness,* (San Francisco, CA: Jossey-Bass, 2004), 69.

[2] Spears and Lawrence, *Practicing Servant* Leadership, 47.

[3] Spears and Lawrence, *Practicing Servant* Leadership, 67.

41

# 10 CORE COMPETENCIES OF SERVANT LEADERSHIP AND PHILANTHROPIC INSTITUTIONS

*"You cannot buy engagement, and you will pay for disengagement."*

~Adele du Rand, Professional speaker[1]

*Servant-Leadership and Philanthropic Institutions* by John C. Burkhardt and Larry C. Spears represent Chapter Five of the book we are using as a guide, *Practicing Servant-Leadership: Succeeding Through Trust, Bravery, and Forgiveness* by Larry C. Spears and Michelle Lawrence.[2]

In this chapter, Burkhardt and Spears discuss the ever-growing and evolving field of philanthropy including the ever-changing society in which these institutions seek to serve. Robert Greenleaf had some ideas about the roles of service and leadership within philanthropic institutions and he believed, as I do, that service and leadership are interdependent, symbiotic and connected.

Burkhardt and Spears mention the characteristics of servant leadership; listening, empathy, healing, persuasion, awareness, foresight, conceptualization, commitment to the growth of the people, stewardship, and building community with regard to and in alignment with philanthropic institutions. Here is a recap of each.

## Listening
Philanthropic institutions must show the way forward and listen not only to themselves but must listen to, and even amplify the voices of those they serve, that go unheard.

## Empathy

Foundations and other grants-making organizations must be ever careful that within their role of judging grant proposals (most times way more than they can fund) that they don't lose sight of the people who have a need. They need to maintain this empathetic connection between the people who have the influence, and the people who are being served.

## Healing

Healing in this context refers to the healing of one's self, first. Greenleaf challenged us to heal internally from the *isms* in the world (racism, sexism, etc.) and to provide access to opportunity, promote and engage in peace, and to build community. He said these efforts cannot happen if we have not addressed them both internally, as well as externally. Indeed, philanthropic institutions have the responsibility in the ongoing process of reconciliation.

## Persuasion

Foundations must rely on leadership that works by influencing people through the power of morality, and not through coercion and positional authority.

## Awareness

Philanthropic institutions must rely more on the awareness of perception to a greater level than ever before. Greenleaf spoke about the leaders as the seeker and in the grants-making world, awareness is a more evolved way to work (and judge grant proposals) rather than to just rely on objectivity, detachment, and expert knowledge. Awareness is at the next level of consciousness than these.

## Foresight

For philanthropic institutions, foresight is the most important servant leadership characteristic to possess. Just as the original donor employs foresight in leaving an endowment for the future of service, the institution must commit to resources in the present, not thinking about the present day but using foresight considering the future of its work and service.

## Conceptualization

Conceptualization is about grant-making institutions making meaning of its work and service to society. In this context, vision and conceptualization are seen as processes in which the leaders and followers arrive at a decision together. Conceptualization should be seen as the way of the institution and not merely a skill of the leader.

## Commitment to the Growth of the People

As philanthropic institutions shift their consciousness from seeing its philanthropic investments as commitments to the people, rather than as the problem, they will perceive their work in a different way, with a new conceptualization. And Greenleaf called this new way of seeing it as a 'high calling.'

## Stewardship

The role of philanthropy is to, as Peter Block said, "hold something in trust for another."[3] What this means is that wealthy individuals give their wealth to trusted organizations to act responsibly in serving and healing the world. Stewardship must directly impact the decisions that institutions make as stewards of endowments. In other words, keep the original vision of the endowment while operating in today's context of need, all for the people.

## Building Community

Philanthropic institutions must work together in purpose and as clear vehicles of internal cohesion if they are to be of service. Greenleaf says it plainly, "Am I connected?" Modern philanthropic institutions are invited to live and work in a holistic and integrated way so that they are, "on the growing edge of the contemporary phase of history but still connected to the main body of people and events."[4] This is what community building is all about—staying connected to the people.

At the end of the day, philanthropic institutions and organizations have the greatest challenge as they serve and heal the world. Their challenge is to set the intention (create a vision) for their communities that go far beyond their approach, and to create access and contact for the people and for organizations. It is all about *engagement*. Burkhardt and Spears put it in this way, "The sense of community envisioned by Greenleaf does not tolerate much self-interest, nor does it provide much in the way of shelter from real relationships, with real people in real situations."[5]

To engagement,
Dr. Crystal

## Notes

[1]  http://www.adeledurand.com/blog/page/6/
[2]  L. C. Spears and M. Lawrence, *Practicing Servant Leadership: Succeeding through trust, bravery, and forgiveness*, (San Francisco, CA: Jossey-Bass, 2004), 71.
[3]  Spears and Lawrence, *Practicing Servant* Leadership, 85.
[4]  Spears and Lawrence, *Practicing Servant* Leadership, 87.
[5]  Spears and Lawrence, *Practicing Servant* Leadership, 88.

*Crystal J. Davis*


## 42

# FOUR VALUES OF SERVANT-LED ORGANIZATIONS


*"There is nothing wrong with creating greater shareholder value or making a profit in your company...However, there is something wrong when a Fortune 500 company doesn't consider that its primary mission should be to exist for the sake of others, and not just for the sake of others in their exclusive shareholder family, but for the sake of making this world to the least and the last a better place."*

> ~ Dr. Tony Baron, *The Art of Servant Leadership*[1]

*On the Right Side of History* by John C. Bogle represents Chapter Six of the book we are using as a guide, *Practicing Servant-Leadership: Succeeding Through Trust, Bravery, and Forgiveness* by Larry C. Spears and Michelle Lawrence.[2]

In this chapter, Bogle provides us with a captivating overview of the Vanguard Group, a mutual fund organization that has, since its inception, used the principles and philosophy of servant-leadership to make it a leader in the mutual fund industry. Bogle argues that Vanguard's principles of creating a corporate environment that encourages its staff to do the right things in the right way, have placed them on the right side of history.

It's fascinating to read the story of the Vanguard Group and how they have surpassed their competitors in the industry by fostering a single focus on serving their fund's shareholders, creating and maintaining an attitude towards low costs, and utilizing conservative investment strategies and concepts. Operating under the servant-leadership philosophy, the Vanguard Group enjoys assets topping of 400 billion, cash flow at 50 billion, and switching to a no-load distribution in 1977; all this made the Vanguard Group that segment's largest unit.

How do they do it?

Bogle takes ideas from Greenleaf's essay, *Building a Model Institution* that provided the wisdom and vision for what has been manifested at the Vanguard Group.[3] Here is a recap of each.

### Distinguished serving institutions
Employees who accept the challenge of discipline to operate in a higher consciousness are lifted to a nobler stature and are more effective. They are likely to achieve greater things with less discipline in the workplace.

### An understanding of leadership and followership
Everyone in any institution is part leader and part follower. It follows that those employees that are natural servant leaders are the ones that should be empowered to lead at all levels of the organization.

### Organizational structure
Organizations that place an importance on organizational structure and culture understand how power and authority are handled. In this way, discipline toward helping employees accomplish their goals for themselves and others, makes for a successful organizational structure. The Vanguard Group places the most power and authority with the fund shareholders rather than with the managers. In essence, the collective power rests in the hands of those Vanguard serves.

### The need for trustees
The Vanguard Group understands the need for trustees, that is, those persons in whom ultimate trust is placed. These persons are objective, unattached people who stand apart from the organization offering a detachment commitment that are known only to insiders.

Not only are the above-mentioned characteristics vital to the success of the Vanguard Group, but so are foresight and caring. Foresight is crucial to leaders to navigate the unknown. Foresight is about operating with a sense of purpose and objective, moving toward and embracing the unknown and harnessing the talent to manage the process for reaching new goals. Finally, the third is to have people who care about the organization.

Bogle puts it this way,

'...the institution must be the object of intense human care and cultivation. Even when it errs and stumbles, it must be cared for, and the burden must be borne by all who work for it, all who own it, and all who are served by it, all who govern it.'[4]

At the end of the day, 'the Vanguard way' is about creating extra value for its investors and indeed, their peers recognize this value advantage. Others in the industry did not pay attention until 10 years after the Vanguard Group's success was noticed. And, they are being copied, but not with much enthusiasm.

Amazing...

Servant leadership is on the right side of evolving corporate history and its policies and procedures, that is, the *consciousness* that Vanguard adopted a quarter-century ago, makes them a valuable servant-led institution today.

To servant-led organizations,
Dr. Crystal

## Notes

[1] T. Baron, *The art of servant leadership*, (Tucson. AZ: Wheatmark Publishers, 2010), 109.

[2] L. C. Spears and M. Lawrence, *Practicing Servant Leadership: Succeeding through trust, bravery, and forgiveness*, (San Francisco, CA: Jossey-Bass, 2004), 91.

[3] R. K. Greenleaf, *The servant as leader*, (Indianapolis, IN: The Robert K. Greenleaf Center, 1970).

[4] Spears and Lawrence, *Practicing Servant Leadership*, 101.

43

# 11 TIPS FOR SERVANT-LEADERSHIP
# COLLABORATIONS

*"When an organization knows its Spirit, it can lead itself from within…Organizations need a strong sense and conscience, a strong awareness of self, who are we? What are we trying to do?"*

~ Margaret Wheatley, *Author of Leadership and the New Science*[1]

*Anatomy of a Collaboration: An Act of Servant-Leadership* by Wendell J. Walls represents Chapter Seven of the book we are using as a guide, *Practicing Servant-Leadership: Succeeding Through Trust, Bravery, and Forgiveness* by Larry C. Spears and Michelle Lawrence.[2]

Wendell J. Walls provides us with a fascinating story of how two organizations came together to host a joint conference (summer of 1999), and how they forged a perfect union, partnership, between themselves, the Greenleaf Centers for Servant Leadership and the Community Leadership organization.[3]

As the old saying goes, "it's all about timing" and as it were, at the time of writing this blog and reading this fascinating story, a board of directors that I belong to, is in its **initial** conversation with another organization (of like-minded souls) to merge conferences. Coincidence, you say? Nope. Everything *always* works together for what you need at the exact and perfect time. I am printing this article to take to the next board meeting.

So, Walls takes us through the journey; how both organizations moved to Indianapolis, how the two CEO's got together (Walls and Larry Spears) and really connected with their organization's work and future, both professionally and personally. He narrates as to how one day during a conversation Spears and Walls had at a pub on the north side of Indianapolis, Spear said, "What do you think about doing a joint conference?" to which Walls replied, "Sounds like a good idea to me." And so was born the idea, *really a new consciousness of collaboration*, between the two organizations.

That's how it happens.

Collaboration is born out of two people or two organizations (or several organizations) who have the same consciousness of servant leadership. Both sides (or all sides) come together and realize that it is all about service. Walls said about the collaboration, "It is my belief that this collaboration reflected a consummate act of servant leadership by the two organizations via their staff and the board leadership."[4] This example provides us, and me in a perfect way, with a model for effective institutional collaboration.

What I really thought was dead on Wall's article is that he talked about how, in the midst of planning, the focus was on whether the two organizations came together because of a finance issue or even if the collaboration was about a merger or take-over. Funny, how the energy of fear always races in first....

But because Walls and Spears and their organizations are both servant-minded in nature, there existed a spirit of congeniality right from the start. And this, my friends, will always take an idea or a thought to the next level. Walls goes on to say how several positive ways of operating assisted the collaboration along the way; meaningful communication, putting the hard stuff in writing early, accepting differences and similarities, navigating crisis together, and facilitation as an equal part of collaboration.

Walls talks about the synchronicity of it all and how successful the conference was. He mentioned the book by Joe Jaworski (I ordered this morning on Amazon) called *Synchronicity*.[5] And I believe, just like Walls does, that the entire collaboration was meant to be, because that's what synchronicity is about, "when things come together in an almost unbelievable way in our lives; high energy, coherence, a deep sense of satisfaction, distributed leadership, and highly significant results."[6] Wow.

I am so excited that I happened to chance upon this article at the exact time that I would need it. I am inspired by the possibility that lies in front of me; to be a part of a collaboration that will, in the end, serve and heal the

161

two organizations themselves and to be a beneficial presence to the people the two organizations serve.

Walls gives us 11 tips when considering collaboration. I'll type this up separately to present to the board. Here is a recap of each.

- Build relationships at every opportunity. These relationships can be the gateway to future collaborative projects.
- Allow the time and space for ideas to come forth. This could be quiet times or *aha* moments. Ideas always come as a result of great communication and listening.
- Collaborate just because it's the right thing to do. There's no need to wait for a problem to occur which then we believe, a collaboration, will solve.
- There will be risks. Take them. No risk, no reward.
- People fear loss, not change. Realizing this early on helps to ease the feelings of loss.
- Frequent face-to-face meetings are a must. Emails, phone calls, and texts alone will not get it.
- Put all of the firm stuff in writing immediately, Then, let the collaboration form organically as you move along.
- Differences are a great path of creativity, discovery, and change. Spend time understanding differences between one another (or between organizations).
- There's nothing better than a crisis to seal a strong collaboration. Don't fear it. Embrace it.
- For the health of the group, engage in facilitation. If there is no independent facilitator, then facilitate for one another.
- If in doubt, charge ahead. It will be worth the effort.

I wrote a blog post about a year and a half ago on collaboration. It was my most-viewed post in the history of my journey to share my message of servant-leadership (2,656 views). That was a clear indication for me that people and organizations realize the importance of collaboration.

I like what Walls spoke on; Stephen Covey's four roles of leadership. Covey talked about them at the conference. He said that the leader must be a model of credibility, diligence, and the spirit of servant leadership; first and foremost, the leadership role is about pathfinding, wherein a vision is discerned, the alignment of values between organizations must be institutionalized, and the fourth role (which is the fruit of the first three) is to empower the people.

I have been fortunate enough to be a part of many community-based and organizationally-based collaboration projects where we empowered the people around an idea. It's hard work. Collaboration is about building relationships. It is about stepping into the unknown together and making dreams come true. Collaborations are about manifesting something into being. They are about leaning into and recognizing synchronicity when it happens. And when it all comes together, oh how sweet it is…

To collaboration,
Dr. Crystal

## Notes

1   M. Wheatley, *Leadership is the new science: Discovering order in a chaotic world.* (San Francisco, CA: Berrett-Koehler Publishers, Inc., 1999), 118.
2   L. C. Spears and M. Lawrence, *Practicing Servant Leadership: Succeeding through trust, bravery, and forgiveness,* (San Francisco, CA: Jossey-Bass, 2004), 113.
3   Spears and Lawrence, *Practicing Servant Leadership*, 113.
4   Spears and Lawrence, *Practicing Servant Leadership*, 115.
5   J. Jaworski, *Synchronicity: The inner path of leadership,* (San Francisco, CA: Berrett-Koehler Publishers, Inc.,1996)
6   Spears and Lawrence, *Practicing Servant Leadership*, 129.

44

# THE EIGHT PITFALLS OF ORGANIZATIONS AND EMERGING SERVANT-LEADERS

*Servant-Leadership Characteristics in Organizational Life* by Don DeGraaf, Colin Tilley, and Larry Neal represents Chapter Eight of the book we are using as a guide, *Practicing Servant-Leadership: Succeeding Through Trust, Bravery, and Forgiveness* by Larry C. Spears and Michelle Lawrence.[1]

These authors provided an overview of the ten core competencies of servant leadership (Larry Spears created), but in this context, they used them in tandem with organizational life. I wrote about the ten core competencies a while back. Rather than go back through them, I would like to touch on the core competencies that resonated with me today, and with another book, I am reading right now, *Synchronicity: The Inner Path to Leadership* by Joseph Jaworski.[2] That core competency is *awareness*. But before I do, we should understand why awareness is so critical. Warren Bennis, Tom Cronin, and Harlan Cleveland suggested eight propositions for American leaders as to what blocks our ability to embrace awareness more fully[3]:

- the trouble with American leaders is their lack of self-knowledge.
- the trouble with American leaders is their lack of appreciation for the nature of leadership itself.
- the trouble with American leaders is their focus on concepts that separate (communities, nations, disciplines, fields, methods, etc.), rather than concepts that express our interconnectedness.
- the trouble with American leaders is their ignorance of the world and of the US Interdependence—their lack of world-mindedness.
- the trouble with American leaders is their inattention to values— forgetting to ask "Why?" and "What for?"

- the trouble with American leaders is that they do not know how to make changes, to analyze 'social architecture' [Warren Bennis's term], and to create a team to make something different happen.
- the trouble with American leaders is an insufficient appreciation of the relevance of stakeholders, of the implications of pluralism, and of the fact that nobody is in charge, and therefore each leader is partly in charge of the situation as a whole.
- the trouble with American leaders is that they are not sufficiently aware of the context, or the external environment, or whatever it is they are responsible for doing.

Wow. These guys really pulled us on the carpet and told us about ourselves. I have seen and continue to learn myself as a servant-leader concerning the criticisms listed above.

Servant-leaders understand that the core competency, *awareness,* is most critical to the development of the inner life of a servant-leader and the impact it has on organizational life. That cliché, "some men go through a forest and see no firewood,' is so true in the ever-changing life of an unaware organization. That lack of awareness is dangerous to the 21st-century organization.

The need for managers to be critically aware of their customers, their staff, and their organization is well researched. But, as servant-leaders know, that additional step is to develop self-awareness. Self-awareness is about realizing life *while* living it, in every moment. As Jaworski says in his book, "it is a fundamental shift of mind."

And the shift is a challenge. Heck, we are *all* so busy. It is easier to live superficially than to live deeply. With all the programs we must develop, people to see, places to go to, and things to do, it's a no wonder we can't get off of the hamster wheel for a moment of self-reflection!

As a part of awareness, self-reflection allows us to renew the passion that attracted us to our organizations in the first place. It is necessary to get that 'fire back in our belly' so that we can access, reflect, and be honest with ourselves if we want to sustain our passion in our workplace and in our personal lives.

I know that I am speaking to the choir right now. As servant-leaders we know all of this stuff. But, it is our responsibility to help others, to help other organizations, to help other boards of directors. And boy, do I have the perfect opportunity in front of me. Have you ever been to a meeting where vital energy in the room is dead? I mean you can hear the crickets chirping and feel the lack of passion. This group that I am a new member of should engage in self-reflection and be honest about where they are. Otherwise, I am afraid of what their destiny will be. They have long lost their passion and the way forward.

I leave you with a passage on the passion that the Spears and Lawrence spoke about; I know that if this group (and others) can get the passion back, they can survive and thrive as market leaders.

"When servant-leaders can demonstrate their passion for the core values of their organization, they reaffirm their organization's commitment to the growth of the people and to building social capital within their communities. As a result, we must continue to develop the 'inner fire within ourselves,' which allows us to continue to deliver programs and services at a high level over the long term, as well as encouraging a passion for services within our staff to meet the needs of the customers."[4]

To re-igniting the fire within,
Dr. Crystal

## Notes

[1] L. C. Spears and M. Lawrence, *Practicing Servant Leadership: Succeeding through trust, bravery, and forgiveness*, (San Francisco, CA: Jossey-Bass, 2004), 133.

[2] J. Jaworski, *Synchronicity: The inner path of leadership*, (San Francisco, CA: Berrett-Koehler Publishers, Inc.,1996)

[3] Jaworski, *Synchronicity*, 96-7

[4] Spears and Lawrence, *Practicing Servant Leadership*, 164.

45

# SIX POSITIVE PHRASES SERVANT-LEADERS USE
# WHEN LISTENING

*"There is a difference between listening and waiting for your turn to speak."*

~Simon Sinek[1]

Since there was so much useful information in Chapter Eight, *Servant-Leadership Characteristics in Organizational Life* by Don De Graaf, Colin Tilley, and Larry Neal, I decided to blog again on this chapter from the book we are using as a guide, *Practicing Servant-Leadership: Succeeding Through Trust, Bravery, and Forgiveness* by Larry C. Spears and Michelle Lawrence.[2]

Of the 10 core competencies of servant-leadership, the foundational competency is listening. Not just listening, but **authentic** listening. That's why it is the first core competency because it serves as the vehicle through which the other competencies can be nurtured. Servant-leaders understand that great leaders are good communicators who can speak eloquently and more efficiently, but they are excellent and empathetic listeners.

One way that servant-leaders can develop listening skills is to practice reflective listening. Reflective listening includes three components:

- **nonverbal clues**: Learning to be aware of nonverbal communication in yourself and in others
- **understanding the content**: Understanding the speaker's main ideas and checking them out
- **understanding feelings**: Listening for and being aware of the feelings a person may have when communicating

And if you are like me, you've had to learn that remarks like, "I see" or "Oh, really?" or "You did?" are noncommittal responses and are not considered reflective or empathetic listening. Door-openers are responses that engage the person who is speaking and makes you an *active* listener. For example, below are some door-opening phrases that are either positive phrases or killer phrases. See if you have ever said any of these phrases.

**Positive Phrases** or **Killer Phrases**

- Keep talking, you're on track.    The problem with that idea…
- Keep going.    It's not a bad idea, but…
- I'm glad you brought that up.    You haven't considered…
- How can we build on that?    We've tried that before.
- That's an interesting idea.    You don't understand the problem.
- Let's try it.    Has anyone else ever tried it?[3]

Servant-leaders understand that when we actively listen and use positive phrases rather than negative ones, we confirm for the listener that we hear and feel what they are saying. And don't we all want to be heard and understood?

My son participated in an assignment this week whereby he brought the *real baby* home. It was a part of his home economics class, the Real Baby Simulation Experience. It was fun. And he was tired. I got the chance to actively listen to him as he was frustrated at certain points of the experience where the baby was fussy. I stayed the course with him and listened quietly.

I offered him suggestions and coached him through it. He told me he could handle the baby through the night. And he did. He never came to get me. The next morning, he was so proud of himself. He did it! And I am proud of him too! He was actively listening for the baby's cry and immediately began figuring out what the baby's needs were. He was attentive and caring.

I always thought he was a loving child. And even as a teenager (and his teenager-ish attitude at times), his compassion, and authentic love showed through in his care and concern for the baby. What a great experience for him…and for me too!

To authentic listening,
Dr. Crystal

*Crystal J. Davis*

## Notes

L. C. Spears and M. Lawrence, *Practicing Servant Leadership: Succeeding through trust, bravery, and forgiveness*, (San Francisco, CA: Jossey-Bass, 2004).

[2] Spears and Lawrence, *Practicing Servant Leadership,* 133.

[3] Spears and Lawrence, *Practicing Servant Leadership*, 137.

46

# FOUR PREMISES OF THEOLOGY CONCERNING SERVANT-LED INSTITUTIONS

*Towards a Theology of Institutions* by David Specht and Richard Broholm represents Chapter Nine of the book we are using as a guide, *Practicing Servant-Leadership: Succeeding Through Trust, Bravery, and Forgiveness* by Larry C. Spears and Michelle Lawrence.[1]

I think it is befitting that after the presidential debate that took place last night, this chapter speaks about this particular moment in time being both a terribly auspicious and an incredibly exciting moment to be exploring servant-leadership and Robert Greenleaf's call for a theology of institutions.[2] While there are innumerable opportunities for leadership to fail, some failures are particularly grievous, for, in each instance, they appear to reflect a fundamental lack of clarity on the part of those in leadership about **what** and **whom** they are holding in trust.

Today, we are facing a level of dispiritedness and lack of confidence in the commitment and capacity of public institutions, private institutions, and leaders that are unmatched. At the same time, is it also an exciting and provocative time to explore the lively intersectionality of the human spirit, sacred tradition, leadership, and institutional life.

Robert Greenleaf realized in the 1970s, the necessity of existing institutions recognizing and adopting servant-leadership as a way of life and leading. We are in desperate need to understand and adopt servant-leadership in our institutions, both socially and politically in today's atmosphere.

To that end, Specht and Broholm offer four theological premises for those who would hold organizations in trust.[3] Let us recap each of these premises.

## Premise 1: Institutions are a part of God's order

Decent humanity and basic human respect are inextricably tied to and not separate from, its social and political institutions.

## Premise 2: God loves institutions

All faith and spiritual traditions understand that God's love is universal and is also the true essence of God's intimate concern for each of us as individuals. Servant-leaders understand that rooting ourselves in the premise that God loves institutions (even in their mess) is an essential basis for the compassionate regard for organizations and institutions that enable us to hold them in trust.

## Premise 3: Institutions are living systems

The affirmative belief that institutions are whole and living systems, allows us to see first that institutions are alive and that they are systems. As such, they are wholly and completely interdependent on the evolving world, both impacting and affecting everything around them. The authors put it this way,

"A fundamental mindfulness discipline of healthy organizations and institutions is maintaining a consistent awareness of these two dimensions of the institution's utter interdependence with the world around it: both its fundamental dependence upon the world and the inevitable intended and unintended consequences of its decisions and actions upon that same world."[4]

## Premise 4: Institutions are called and gifted, they are fallen, and they are capable of being redeemed

These premises hold three important theological assertions concerning the nature of institutions that stand in their own right and are interdependent on one another. As called and gifted institutions, they are called here for a reason. They are intended to represent instruments of God's healing and reconciliation and to serve the common good, and good things are expected of them. Institutions are fallen and prone to inflating themselves, displaying disrespect and forgetfulness for their membership, and act in ways that neglect or harm the common good. In this way, institutions are capable of both great good and immeasurable harm.

Fundamentally speaking, holding an institution in trust, particularly around its brokenness, and in recognition of the realities mentioned above- is to acknowledge that it is gifted and that it is capable of being re-awakened to its absolute best and evolved consciousness for the good of its people. Each of these premises can coexist simultaneously as possibilities within the life of institutions, each presenting in great measure, at any given moment in the life of an organization.

To human decency and respect for one another,
Dr. Crystal

## Notes

[1] L. C. Spears and M. Lawrence, *Practicing Servant Leadership: Succeeding through trust, bravery, and forgiveness*, (San Francisco, CA: Jossey-Bass, 2004), 167.
[2] Spears and Lawrence, *Practicing Servant Leadership*, 1.
[3] Spears and Lawrence, *Practicing Servant Leadership*, 181 84.
[4] Spears and Lawrence, *Practicing Servant Leadership*, 184.

47

# SERVANT LEADERSHIP AND FORGIVENESS

*"On the horizon of this landscape, a landscape that is personal and spiritual as it is political and global, we see ourselves free of what binds us, and we walk in such a way that others are drawn forward so that they too, may be free."*

~Shann Ferch[1]

*Servant-Leadership, Forgiveness, and Social Justice* by Shann R. Ferch represents Chapter Eleven of the book we are using as a guide, *Practicing Servant-Leadership: Succeeding Through Trust, Bravery, and Forgiveness* by Larry C. Spears and Michelle Lawrence.[2]

Servant-leaders understand the concept of forgiveness and with each new day work towards the consciousness of forgiveness of one's own shortcomings and the shortcomings of others so that they may see the heart of people in everyday living. Forgiveness is paramount to the servant-leader as it improves relationships of all kinds and types and brings out the best in people.

The on-going expansiveness and unfolding of a servant-leader are that they desire to honor all of the relationships that they are involved with and see those relationships as sacred. I certainly appreciate how the author combines the construct of forgiveness with servant leadership and social justice.

I believe Dr. Ferch hit the nail on the head when he argued that the more traditional ways of leading fail to take into account people's emotional and spiritual wellbeing. BAM! These types of leaders fail to consider their **own** emotional and spiritual well-being much less than anyone else's and this type of atmosphere (culture) is a breeding ground for the elitist mentality. In the end, these leaders, however well meaning, end up leading from a different energy than from the heart of a serving leader.

This is where servant leadership can help. Organizationally speaking, Ferch puts it this way, "the idea of servant-leadership...can be seen in movements that have brought dead organizations back to life, and reconciliation and healing to nations deeply wounded by human atrocities."[3]

Other noted scholars in servant leadership acknowledge that as a part of this sacredness, just as Greenleaf did, listening is paramount to the servant-leader. Listening aligns behavior and cognition with everyday activities and is most effective when connecting with others and involves a give-and-take relationship. Through the act of listening and providing feedback, relationships develop and mature, creating more servant-leaders.

Kouzes and Posner found that empathy is critical to effective leadership; along with listening, empathy, and trust, servant-leaders make organizations functional and influence others within the organization.[4] Greenleaf claimed servant-leaders have an unqualified acceptance and a tolerance of imperfection.[5] Empathy allows the followers to expand consciousness and recognize their acceptance for who they are. Taken together, listening, empathy and trust allow servant-leaders to facilitate relationships and demonstrate attributes such as trust, integrity, accountability, and authentic concern for people.[6]

Empathy, listening, and meaningful dialogue is critical for servant-leaders developing a higher, more evolved consciousness that seeks to heal one's self and others so that the servant-leader is better and by extension, the organization in which they work.

What can be found as a result of empathy, listening, and meaningful dialogue is reconciliation, as Ferch says, "...the deeper restoration that is the result of a disciplined and unflinching look at the wrongs we do to one another."[7]

Ferch is **so** right when he argued that servant-leaders can invigorate organizations through a culture of acceptance, empathy, and relational justice. More than that, when this energy is present, forgiveness is a part of the cultural landscape of the organization where it can be asked for and granted, and the servant-leader models such behavior.

Phew! Powerful stuff, right?

At the end of the day, if we, as servant-leaders, can incorporate these ideas into our thinking and heart space, we can create and sustain joy for ourselves and others. Moreover, most certainly, we can create this in our organizations (where we spend so much of our daily lives) so that we work with joy, calling to a higher purpose, and personal meaning. In this way, we all are free.

To forgiveness,
Dr. Crystal

## Notes

[1] L. C. Spears and M. Lawrence, *Practicing Servant Leadership: Succeeding through trust, bravery, and forgiveness*, (San Francisco, CA: Jossey-Bass, 2004),239.

[2] Spears and Lawrence, *Practicing Servant Leadership*, 225.

[3] Spears and Lawrence, *Practicing Servant Leadership*, 228.

[4] Crystal J. Davis, *Self-transcendence and servant leadership behavior in new thought spiritual centers: A correlational study*, (University of Phoenix, ProQuest Dissertations Publishing, 2014. 3691408), 44.

[5] Davis, *Self-transcendence and servant leadership*, 44.

[6] Davis, *Self-transcendence and servant leadership*, 44.

[7] Spears and Lawrence, *Practicing Servant Leadership*, 235.

# 48

# SERVANT LEADERSHIP: THE MOVEMENT

*"Despite current ads and slogans, the world doesn't change one person at a time. It changes when networks of relationships form among people who share a common cause and vision of what's possible. This is good news for those of us intent on creating a positive future. Rather than worry about critical mass, our work is to foster critical connections. We don't need to convince large numbers of people to change; instead, we need to connect with kindred spirits. Through these relationships, we will develop the new knowledge, practices, courage and commitment that lead to broad-based change."*

~Margaret Wheatley[1]

*The Servant-Leader: From Hero to Host* by Margaret J. Wheatley represents the last chapter, Chapter Twelve of the book we are using as a guide, *Practicing Servant-Leadership: Succeeding Through Trust, Bravery, and Forgiveness* by Larry C. Spears and Michelle Lawrence.[2]

Margaret Wheatley, author of the book, *Leadership, and the New Science: Discovering Order in a Chaotic World* sums up the servant leadership experience in her interview with Larry Spears and John Noble of the Greenleaf Center for Servant Leadership in the last chapter of the book. I believe her words and hope sustains and drives the servant leadership movement forward. Here are her closing remarks.

"We are the ones we've been waiting for. That phrase comes from a wonderful gospel song. This is the time for which we have been preparing, and so there is a deep sense of call. Servant leadership is not just an interesting idea but something fundamental and vital for the world, something the world truly does need. The concept of servant leadership must move from an interesting idea in the public imagination toward the realization that *this is the only way we can go forward.*" I personally experience that sense of right-timelessness to this body of work called servant leadership. I feel that for more and more of us, we need to realize that it will take even more courage to move forward, but that the necessity of moving forward is clear. It moves from being a body of work to being a movement—literally a movement—how we are going to move in this world. I think that will require more acts of courage, more clarity, more saying this has to change now. I am hoping that it will change now.[3]

Servant-leaders understand that leadership is a journey and that servant leadership is a movement whose time has come. We are here to live, learn, and lead with a heart of service. I wish you the very best for your servant leadership journey!

To the movement,
Dr. Crystal

## Notes

[1]  https://www.kosmosjournal.org/contributor/margaret-wheatley/
[2]  L. C. Spears and M. Lawrence, *Practicing Servant Leadership: Succeeding through trust, bravery, and forgiveness*, (San Francisco, CA: Jossey-Bass, 2004), 241.
[3]  Spears and Lawrence, *Practicing Servant Leadership*, 268.

49

# LEAD FROM WITHIN LEARNING BLOG: 2016 YEAR IN REVIEW

*"Lead a More Daring Life"*

~David Berry[1]

It has been an amazing year for my learning blog, **Lead.From.Within.** The three-year journey has been full of amazing learning experiences, networking opportunities and the chance to teach and write about servant leadership. This year, my message has spanned across 69 places in the world, the top five including the United States, Brazil, Canada, Philippines, and Russia! That is 31 more places than last year! I am truly grateful for the opportunity to share this journey with you.

I want to share seven contemplation questions that Cynthia James (https://cynthiajames.net/) challenged us to sit with and to journal the answers at the beginning of this year. However, first let's take a quick glance back at what we have learned and the tools we have gained for our servant leadership tool box in 2016:

**Two books**

1. *A Force for Good: The Dalai Lama's Vision for Our World* by Daniel Goleman.
2. *Practicing Servant-Leadership: Succeeding Through Trust, Bravery, and Forgiveness* by Larry C. Spears and Michelle Lawrence

**Themes**

The themes from *A Force for Good* included the key concepts below.

1. Free the mind and heart

2. Embody compassion
3. Educate the heart
4. Oppose injustice
5. Choose humane economics
6. Help those in need
7. Heal the earth
8. Connect across divides

The themes from *Practicing Servant Leadership* were varied, including servant leadership and boards of directors, servant leadership and organizations, and the use of positive language as servant-leaders.

## Bloggers

Four bloggers/teachers that have challenged me to greater depths of service and spirituality are David Berry[3], Marcel Schwantes[4], Cynthia James[5], and Rosetta Thurman[6]. If you have a chance, you should check them out.

Cynthia James, a poet, novelist, and independent scholar posted a challenge for us on Facebook. She had presented seven contemplation questions for us to consider for our lives in 2017. When you have a chance, take some time to contemplate and jot your answers down. She says that if we listen for 30 days (at least 10 minutes a day), we shall see amazing results in our lives! Here they are:

1. What is the highest vision for my life?
2. What must be released to fulfill this vision?
3. What makes my heart sing?
4. Where can I be of service that makes a difference?
5. Who is the people that inspire me and why? How am I like those people?
6. Where are the places I made a difference this year?
7. If there were no obstacles. What would I be doing?

In the coming year, I will continue to ask myself the following questions (last year's contemplation questions) and I ask you to do the same:

1. How can I serve?
2. How can you serve?
3. How can we serve together?
4. Under what context am I serving?
5. What do I want the end result of my service to look like?

I thank each of you wholeheartedly for your support of my blog! I am indeed in a debt of gratitude to you. I look forward with great joy and anticipation for our work together. All is well. We are complete. And so it is. Namaste.

*"Something extraordinary is waiting for you."*

To our journey,
Dr. Crystal

## Notes

[1] https://rule13learning.com/
[2] https://rule13learning.com/ - David Berry
[3] https://www.inc.com/author/marcel-schwantes – Marcel Schwantes
[4] https://www.cynthiajames.net/ - Cynthia James
[5] https://happyblackwoman.com/ - Rosetta Thurman

# SELECT SERVANT LEADERSHIP ESSAYS

*Crystal J. Davis*

## 50

# SERVANT LEADERSHIP AND EMPLOYEE EMPOWERMENT

*"Organizations that empower folks further down the chain or try to get rid of the big hierarchal chains and allow decision making to happen on a more local level end up being more adaptive and resilient because there are more minds involved in the problem."*

~Steven Johnson[1]

Servant-leaders choose to empower individuals and teams. In the workplace, it is critical that servant-leaders enable employees to think, behave, and take the appropriate actions to control their work and to make decisions as independent, autonomous individuals. This power encourages employees to take control of their own destiny-at work and in their personal lives.

Empowerment can be defined as allowing people to make choices that transfer into desired outcomes and to achieve influence within an organization. It has also been called **participative management**.

So, we must be clear that empowerment is not seen as what servant-leaders **do** for their employees. If empowerment is thought of from this perspective, generally speaking, employees would **wait** until empowerment is bestowed upon them by a manager or leader rather than acting and behaving from an empowered position of authority.

When servant-leaders encourage, involve, and enable their employees, the organizational benefits include:

- improved customer satisfaction
- improved delivery of service
- increased creativity and innovation

183

- increased productivity, and
- increased competitive advantage for the organization.

From a servant-leader perspective, there are 10 key values for empowering one's employees:

### Value people

Servant-leaders are mindful that how they feel about people can be seen and felt through their everyday actions and words. Body language (verbal and non-verbal) expresses your consciousness about the people who report to you. A servant-leader appreciates each individual's unique value and contribution, irrespective of an employee's ability to perform a task. Visibility of a servant-leader's appreciation and respect of employees are the key.

### Share the organization's vision

Servant-leaders make sure that everyone in the organization understands and is committed to the mission, vision, and strategic plans of the organization. These leaders walk the walk and talk the talk regarding the overall mission of the organization. Employees who feel that they are part of something bigger than themselves and their individual job, tend to play a more committed role to the organization and the world.

### Trust your employees

Trust is the key word in the workplace. Servant-leaders **intentionally** trust that their team will make the right decision, do the right thing, and act with humility. When leaders trust first, employees feel that and act accordingly. This is the path to gaining trust. Servant-leaders trust to be trusted.

### Share information

Servant-leaders do not hoard information. As a matter of fact, allowing employees access to information allows employees the ability to make thoughtful and sound decisions. Information sharing from leaders assures employees that their thought about what is in the best interest of the organization, is valued and appreciated.

## Give authority away and not just more work
Employees grow and develop new skills when they are given authority and creativity to handle more than just the busy work. Servant-leaders delegate important meetings, projects, and committee work that impact product development and the latter, customers notice. It's all about letting your people shine.

## Provide positive feedback
One of the most important goals of feedback is reward and recognition. Employees want to know how they are doing, and they deserve constructive feedback. Servant-leaders realize the importance of talking to employees, praising them as well as reviewing their performance while honoring the person.

## Look at problems, not people
Problems on the job are related to systems and not to people. Servant-leaders understand that if there is a problem in the workplace, the first thought is to look at the work system. What in the system caused employees to fail? How can the system be adjusted to promote the success of the employee? Servant-leaders always choose to address the problem and not bash the person.

## Look, learn, listen, ask
Servant-leaders know that listening is one of the core competencies of this style of leadership. They guide conversations by not telling grown-up adults what to do but seek employees to provide the right answers. Generally speaking, employees know what the right answer is; they just need the opportunity to reveal it. When problems arise, the servant-leader asks, "What do you think you should do to solve the problem?" or "What steps do you recommend for a healthy resolution?"

**Recognize and reward empowered behavior**

When employees are rewarded for empowered behavior, organizations get more from their employees; energy, commitment, creativity, and fun. The list is endless on the amount of give-back employees will engage in when they feel compensated for the work they do when they are noticed, praised, and appreciated. Servant-leaders know, beyond the shadow of a doubt that when the basic needs of the employee are met, they will give that extra effort voluntarily to their work.

At the end of the day, servant-leaders invest in their employees and in the organization. Indeed, it is their responsibility to create and sustain a work environment where employees act and behave in empowered ways. Servant-leaders are mindful of the barriers that inhibit empowered thinking, and they work to remove them. Empowered employees create a workplace of joy.

To empowerment,
Dr. Crystal

## Notes

[1] https://www.brainyquote.com/quotes/steven_johnson_527635

*Crystal J. Davis*

# 51

# THE NEXT RIGHT MOVE

*"This is what I know for sure; I am here to raise the consciousness of the planet."*

~Oprah Winfrey[1]

As I was thinking about what to write about today, I came across Oprah Winfrey's talk at Stanford University's Graduate School of Business, *"Oprah Winfrey on Career, Life, and Leadership."*[2] Wow. Talk about a fascinating story of servant leadership!

It was the most powerful hour of enlightenment that I have possibly ever experienced. She is the epitome of a servant-leader.

Last week, I talked about the 10 core competencies of servant leadership. Oprah's talk echoed those competencies as she spoke about her life, her career, her mistakes, her successes, and what she has learned from each one of them.

What I took away from the talk was the greatest lesson of all for emerging servant-leaders; servant-leaders who are self-actualized **know** the changes they can make in the world. They are here to raise the consciousness of the planet.

Let that truth soak in for a moment.

Oprah reminded us of the truth of who we are. She said:

- always listen to your inner voice.
- being fuels doing, not the other way around.
- pay attention to your life and to the lives of others.
- work on yourself; always keep yourself full first.
- know who you are and know what to do with who you are.

Isn't this the life and calling of servant-leaders? We are called to be keenly self-aware so that we can make a beneficial contribution to the

187

greater world community. Without knowing who we are, we fail to help others see who they are.

Indeed, servant-leaders understand that there is, as Oprah said, "a supreme moment of destiny waiting for me." Know it. Feel it. *Own* it.

Take an hour in this or in the next 24 hours to watch the talk.

I promise you will feel empowered and inspired to continue on your journey as a servant-leader. It is located at http://bit.ly/12Dnh0C

To Oprah,
Dr. Crystal

## Notes

[1] https://www.youtube.com/watch?v=DEvenWkbZw0
[2] https://www.youtube.com/watch?v=DEvenWkbZw0

52

# 10 CORE COMPETENCIES OF SERVANT LEADERSHIP

*"The role of a servant leader is to stimulate what is already within the person."*

~Dr. Tony Baron, *The Art of Servant Leadership*[1]

Servant-leaders strive to become the best leaders possible each and every day. To do so means that they follow and are empowered by key characteristics that build a service-oriented consciousness (mind-set).

Much of the research on servant-leadership discusses the characteristics of a servant-leader. Some researchers say servant leadership is seen as a confluence of vision, influence, credibility, and trust.

Others include emotional healing, creating value for the community, conceptual skills, empowering, helping subordinates grow and succeed, putting subordinates first, behaving ethically, building and honoring relationships, and servanthood as key characteristics.

One of my favorite researchers, K. Patterson, added another characteristic-love.[2] She defined it as to do goodwill for another.

As we know, Larry Spears defined 10 core competencies for servant-leaders.[3] These competencies are the basis on which all other research, writings, and books on servant leadership are founded.

**1. Authentic Listening** – The servant-leader understands the will of a team and clarifies that will. The servant-leader is always listening with an open heart to what is being said and not said. The servant-leader hears one's own inner voice with reflection and contemplation. This is critical to an emerging servant-leader.

**2. Empathy** – The servant-leader shows empathy and understanding with others. Individuals are accepted and recognized for their unique energy. The servant-leader sees the good intentions of people and does not reject them as people, even when certain behaviors or performance are deemed inappropriate. Servant-leaders are skilled empathetic listeners.

**3. Healing** – Servant-leaders seek wholeness in themselves and others.

**4. Self-Awareness** – Servant-leaders seek awareness at all levels and particularly in issues involving ethics, power, and values. Their view is integrative and holistic.

**5. Persuasion** – Persuasion is seen as a way to convince others, not through positional authority or compliance through coercive tactics. Persuasion in this manner distinguishes the leadership between the authoritarian model and the servant-leadership model. Servant-leaders are effective at building group consensus.

**6. Conceptualization** – Servant-leaders always seek to conceptualize challenges, thinking from a holistic and broad perspective. They dream big and use systemic thinking to approach day-to-day operations. Servant-leaders are forward thinkers, seeking balance between dream and daily life.

**7. Foresight** – Servant-leaders use strategic intuition in thinking and behaviors. Foresight is intuition based on the past, the present, and on the future decision-making process. Foresight is known within the intuitive mind.

**8. Stewardship** – Servant-leaders are good stewards and are concerned for individuals, organizations, and for the world at large. Servant-leaders make good use of all that is given to them and understand stewardship from a global perspective.

**9. Commitment to the Growth of the People** – Servant-leaders are concerned about the growth of the people and as such, encourage and empower personal and professional growth of individuals and teams.

**10. Building Community** – Servant-leaders enjoy building community among people and teams. In organizations, building community means bringing people together around a cause (whatever that cause may be) and developing that community with other organizations and institutions.

Indeed, developing and perfecting these competencies does not happen overnight. But, an emerging servant-leader understands and behaves in a manner consistent with getting better and better with each leadership opportunity.

**Food for Thought;** Gabriel Cousen, the author of *Conscious Eating,* said, *"Joy is the key to everything."*[4] He said that we must live in a way that remembers that truth, including creating a joyful work situation. Isn't that in perfect alignment with servant leadership? This week contemplate on what brings you joy…and *be* that!

To core competencies,
Dr. Crystal

## Notes

[1] Tony Baron, *The art of servant leadership: designing your organization for the sake of others,* (Tucson. AZ: Wheatmark Publishers, 2010).

[2] K. Patterson, Servant leadership: A theoretical model, *ProQuest Dissertations & Theses database,* (2003), UMI No. 3082717.

[3] https://www.regent.edu/acad/global/publications/jvl/vol1_iss1/Spears_Final.pdf

[4] G. Cousen, *Conscious eating.* (Berkeley, CA: North Atlantic Books, 2000), 11.

*Crystal J. Davis*

## 53

## SERVANT LEADERSHIP AND KINDNESS

*"You cannot do a kindness too soon, for you never know how soon it will be too late."*

~Ralph Waldo Emerson[1]

Servant-leaders exemplify the willingness to show kindness and compassion towards others. Servant-leaders attract and keep followers because people believe that they have their best interest at heart.

They understand that if people do not see authentic and genuine empathy in their leader, they will automatically be less trusting.

Just recently, I was given some news that was disheartening and sad for me.

I didn't see it coming, and I did not anticipate it.

This is what change is all about. I heard a talk just a few weeks ago that prepared me for this upcoming change. Rev. Alan Vukas spent a month talking about the key areas in Neale Donald Walsch's book, *When Everything Changes, Change Everything.*[2]

Walsch's nine points about change can help you (as it has for me) to deal with navigating through change are:

- change your decision to 'do it alone,'
- change your choice of emotions,
- change your choice of thoughts,
- change your choice of truths,
- change your idea about change itself,
- change your idea about why change occurs,
- change your idea about future change,
- change your idea about life.
- change your identity.

These key points are valuable for me right now. One's emotional position while embracing change can be a life saver or a deal breaker .

Do you walk around and sulk, mad at the world? Or do you embrace change with kindness?

Much can be said for using kindness while navigating seemingly rough change. Behaviors that can build kindness competencies include:

- listening thoroughly,
- responding patiently to other's frustrations,
- being friendly,
- caring about how others are feeling,
- forgiving others,
- helping to resolve the conflict if you can,
- fostering a positive environment— whether at home or work, and
- always, always, always serving others.

Navigating change in, through, and as kindness is work. One must be silent and disciplined verbally and mentally to what's happening. Servant-leaders who are humble are exceptionally aware of how their emotions can affect change.

Two of the ways that a servant-leader can embrace change is through **acute self-awareness** and most of all seeing and understanding the emotional make-up of others.

Change is inevitable.

How you deal with it determines the outcome. All is well. We are complete. And so it is.

"Something extraordinary is waiting for you."

To change,
Dr. Crystal

## Notes

1 https://www.brainyquote.com/quotes/ralph_waldo_emerson_106295

2  N. D. Walsch, *When everything changes, change everything*, (Ashland, OR: Emnin Books, 2009).

3  N. D. Walsch, *When everything changes, change everything*, 7.

# REFERENCES

Baron, T. (2010). *The art of servant leadership.* (2010). Tucson. AZ: Wheatmark Publishers.

Clifton, D. and Nelson, P. (1992). *Soar with your strengths: A simple yet revolutionary philosophy of business and management.* New York, NY: Dell Publishing.

Cousen, G. (2000). *Conscious eating.* Berkeley, CA: North Atlantic Books.

Covey, S. M. R. (2006). *The speed of trust: The one thing that changes everything.* New York, NY: Free Press.

Davis, C. (2015). *Leading from within: The spirituality of servant leadership.* Saarbrücken, Germany: Lambert Academic Publishing.

Greenleaf, R. K. (1970). *The servant as leader.* Indianapolis, IN: The Robert K. Greenleaf Center.

Goleman, D. (2015). *A force for good: The Dalai Lama's vision for our world.* New York, NY: Bantam Books.

Hayes, M. A. and Comer, M. D. (2010). *Start with humility: Lessons from America's quiet CEO's on how to build trust and inspire followers.* Westfield, IN: Greenleaf Center for Servant Leadership.

Jaworski, J. (1996). *Synchronicity: The inner path of leadership.* San Francisco, CA: Berrett-Koehler Publishers, Inc.

Kim, D. (2002). *Foresight as the central ethic of leadership.* Atlanta, GA: The Greenleaf Center for Servant-Leadership.

Myss, C. (2004). *Invisible acts of power: Channeling grace in your everyday life.* New York, NY: Atria Paperback.

Patterson, K. (2003). *Servant leadership: A theoretical model.* (Doctoral dissertation) Retrieved from ProQuest Dissertations & Theses database. (UMI No. 3082717)

Piketty, T. and Goldhammer, A. (2014*). Capital in the 21st century.* Cambridge, MA: President and Fellows of Harvard College.

Showkeir, J. and Showkeir, M. (2008). *Authentic conversations: Moving from manipulation to truth and commitment.* San Francisco, CA: Berrett-Koehler Publishers, Inc.

Sipe, J. W. and Frick, D. M. (2009). *Seven pillars of servant leadership: Practicing the wisdom of leading by serving.* Mahwah, NJ: Paulist Press.

Spears, L. C. and Lawrence, M. (2004). *Practicing Servant Leadership: Succeeding through trust, bravery, and forgiveness.* San Francisco, CA: Jossey-Bass.

Walsch, N. D. (2009). *When everything changes, change everything.* Ashland, OR: Emnin Books.

*Crystal J. Davis*

Wheatley, M. (1999). *Leadership is the new science: Discovering order in a chaotic world.* San Francisco, CA: Berrett-Koehler Publishers, Inc.

Winfrey, O. (2014). *What I know for sure.* New York, NY: Hearst-Communications.

*Crystal J. Davis*

# SUGGESTED/ADDITIONAL READING

Anderson, U. S. (1954). *Three magic words.* New York, NY: Thomas Nelson & Sons.

Bandura, A. (1985). *Explorations in self-efficacy.* Tokyo: Kaneko-Shoho.

Baron, T. (2010). *The art of servant Leadership: Designing your organization for the sake of others.* Tucson, AZ: Wheatmark.

Bass, B. M., & Bass, R. (2008). *The Bass handbook of leadership: Theory, research & managerial applications* (4th ed.). New York, NY: Free Press.

Berry, D. (2016). *A more daring life. Finding voice at the crossroads of change.* USA: David Berry.

Blanchard, K. (1999). *The heart of a leader: Insights on the art of influence.* Tulsa, OK: Honor Books.

Block, P. (2013). *Stewardship: Choosing service over self-interest.* San Francisco, CA: Berrett-Kohler Publishers, Inc.

Bulkeley, K. (2005). *The wondering brain: Thinking about religion with and beyond cognitive neuroscience.* New York, NY: Routledge, Taylor& Francis Group.

Dalai Lama XIV, H. H. (1999). *Ethics for a new millennium.* New York, NY: Putnam.

Duggan, W. (2007). *Strategic intuition: The creative spark in human achievement.* New York, NY: Columbia University Press.

Frankl, V. E. (1959). *Man's search for meaning: An introduction to logotherapy* (3rd Ed.) New York, NY: Simon & Schuster.

Greenleaf, R. K. (1970). *The servant as leader.* Indianapolis, IN: The Robert K. Greenleaf Center.

Greenleaf, R. K. (1977). *Servant leadership: A journey into the nature of legitimate power and greatness.* New York, NY: Paulist Press.

Greenleaf, R. K. (1996). *On becoming a servant leader: The private writings of Robert K. Greenleaf.* San Francisco, CA: Jossey-Bass, Inc.

Greenleaf, R. K. (1998). *Servant: Retrospect and respect.* In L. C. Spears (Ed.), *The power of servant leadership: Essays* (pp. 17-59). San Francisco, CA: Berrett-Koehler.

Hickman, G. (2016). *Leading organizations: Perspectives for a new era* (3rd ed.). Thousand Oaks, CA: Sage Publications.

Holmes, E. (1966). *Science of mind: A philosophy, a faith, a way of life.* New York, NY: Penguin Putnam, Inc.

Kofman, F. (2013). *Conscious business: How to build value through values.* Boulder, CO: Sounds True, Inc.

Maxwell, J. C. (2012). *The 15 invaluable laws of growth: Live them and reach your potential.* New York, NY: Hatchette Book Group.

O'Malley, E. & Cebula, A. (2015). *Your leadership edge: Lead anytime, anywhere.* Wichita, KS: KLC Press.

Seale, E. (1971). *Take off from within.* Marina del Rey, CA; DeVorss & Company.

Senge, P. (2006). *The fifth discipline: The art & practice of the learning organization.* New York, NY: Double Day.

The Arbinger Institute (2009). *Leadership and self-deception: Getting out of the box.* San Francisco, CA: Berrett-Kohler Publishers, Inc.

# AUTHOR BIOGRAPHY

As an expert servant- leadership consultant, author, and independent Certified Coach, Teacher, and Speaker with the John Maxwell Team, Crystal brings an 'others-centered' approach to helping great leaders build great organizations. Crystal's consulting practice, CJD Consulting Solutions, LLC is a firm that helps organizations and leaders to improve business results by empowering authentic conversations, encouraging members at all levels of the organization to build trust, awareness and meaningful contribution.

From working with leaders to working with teams and individuals, Crystal helps people to envision the future of their organization, coaches them to harness the skills needed to think future-forward and assesses the organizational culture to develop frameworks that will create high performing teams. Crystal considers the comprehensive scope of an organization and its people.

Crystal is the author of two books, *Leading from Within: The Spirituality of Servant Leadership* (2014), *Leadership and Followership: Examining the Impact on Workplace Behavior* (2017). Her research interests are in the areas of servant leadership, organizational development and culture, change management, and diversity in management.

Crystal holds a BA in Journalism and Mass Communications from Kansas State University, an MHR in Human Relations from the University of Oklahoma, and a Doctorate in Management specializing in Organizational Leadership from the University of Phoenix. Her mission is, "I help individuals, organizations, and teams by inviting transformative change in mindset and consciousness because leading always begins within."

# *Thank you!*

Thank you for reading my book. I appreciate your feedback, and I would love to hear what you have to say! I need your input to make the next version of this book and also my future books, better. Please leave me a helpful review on Amazon, letting me know your thoughts!

~ Crystal J. Davis

## CJD Consulting Solutions, LLC

*We help individuals, organizations, and teams by inviting transformative change in mindset and consciousness because leading always begins within.*

**CJD Consulting Solutions, LLC** was founded by Crystal J. Davis in 2004 to fulfill this promise. Our consulting, coaching, training, speaking, and writing are designed to help teams and individuals to accomplish transformative change. We work solely from the perspective of servant leadership.

CJD Consulting Solutions, LLC is an organizational development and leadership consulting firm that uses the servant-leadership approach to link and align organizational performance and for sustainable success.

We believe that empowering and inspiring individuals, teams, and organizations result in enhanced performance and transform and build transformative organizations. We engage in deep listening, we ask powerful questions, and we assess an organization's culture.

At CJD Consulting, we collaborate with leaders and teams to define their vision and blueprint their future success. We work to create meaningful contribution for every person. It is servant leadership. Every day. In every way.

At CJD Consulting Solutions, LLC:

- We develop relationships with our clients based on mutual respect, trust, and individualized attention. We collaborate with you every step of the process.
- We understand that successful organizations execute business acumen and encourage the employee's desire to contribute to something larger

than themselves. We offer innovative frameworks that increase self-awareness and accountability directly improving business results.

- Our work together will challenge you in ways that invite individuals and teams to look within and examine one's thinking, confront reality, and learn tools and frameworks for inner transformation and organizational change. This work is hard work but delivers sustainable results.
- With years of experience in helping businesses and nonprofit organizations to find comprehensive solutions, we tell you the truth if our expertise seems redundant; we confront difficult issues with goodwill.

Our commitment to results is always backed with a guarantee. If we don't deliver the agreed-upon-results, or you do not find value in our work, you do not pay our fees. Plain and simple.

# More books by Crystal J. Davis on Amazon

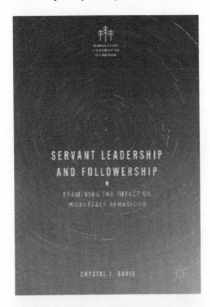

**Leading From Within: The Spirituality of Servant Leadership**

*Crystal J. Davis*

CJD Consulting Solutions, LLC
PO Box 141
Junction City, KS 66441
(785) 317-0045
www.cjdconsultingsolutions.com
crystal@cjdconsultingsolutions.com

CALL CJD CONSULTING, LLC

(785) 317-0045

Made in the USA
Columbia, SC
08 April 2019